REVISE EDEXCEL GCSE (9–1)

History
THE REIGNS OF KING RICHARD I AND KING JOHN, 1189–1216

REVISION
GUIDE AND WORKBOOK

Series Consultant: Harry Smith

Author: Kirsty Taylor

A note from the publisher

In order to ensure that this resource offers high-quality support for the associated Pearson qualification, it has been through a review process by the awarding body. This process confirms that this resource fully covers the teaching and learning content of the specification or part of a specification at which it is aimed. It also confirms that it demonstrates an appropriate balance between the development of subject skills, knowledge and understanding, in addition to preparation for assessment.

Endorsement does not cover any guidance on assessment activities or processes (e.g. practice questions or advice on how to answer assessment questions), included in the resource nor does it prescribe any particular approach to the teaching or delivery of a related course.

While the publishers have made every attempt to ensure that advice on the qualification and its assessment is accurate, the official specification and associated assessment guidance materials are the only authoritative source of information and should always be referred to for definitive guidance.

Pearson examiners have not contributed to any sections in this resource relevant to examination papers for which they have responsibility.

Examiners will not use endorsed resources as a source of material for any assessment set by Pearson.

Endorsement of a resource does not mean that the resource is required to achieve this Pearson qualification, nor does it mean that it is the only suitable material available to support the qualification, and any resource lists produced by the awarding body shall include this and other appropriate resources.

For the full range of Pearson revision titles across KS2, KS3, GCSE, Functional Skills, AS/A Level and BTEC visit:
www.pearsonschools.co.uk/revise

Contents

....

A small bit of small print
Edexcel publishes Sample Assessment Material and the Specification on its website. This is the official content and this book should be used in conjunction with it. The questions in *Now try this* have been written to help you practise every topic in the book. Remember: the real exam questions may not look like this.

The feudal hierarchy

From 1189 to 1216, the dominant feature of English society, especially in the countryside, was the **feudal system**. Each rank of the feudal hierarchy was granted land from the rank above in return for loyalty and service. The king was at the top, with vast power over the whole system.

1 King
The king was extremely powerful. He owned all the land in England but granted most of it to tenants-in-chief. It was his duty to protect his people from invasion and enforce his laws.

2 Tenants-in-chief
Tenants-in-chief were vassals of the king. Most were nobles and important clergy, such as bishops. In return for their fief, they paid homage and provided knight service to the king. The most powerful nobles and clergy were called barons. They advised the king and helped govern England. They granted some of their land to under-tenants.

3 Under-tenants
Under-tenants were vassals to tenants-in-chief. Most were knights and lesser clergy. In return for their land, they paid homage to their lord and provided knight service. Under-tenants granted some of their land to peasants. Most knights were lords of a manor.

The feudal hierarchy

(pyramid labels: King / Tenants-in-chief / Under-tenants / Free men and peasants)

To read about homage, turn to page 2.

4 Free men
Free men could travel and work wherever they wanted. They included merchants, craftsmen and farmers. Free men in villages had to obey and pay rent to their lord, who could be an under-tenant, tenant-in-chief or the king himself. They sometimes worked on their lord's land, but were paid for this.

5 Peasants
Unfree peasants provided labour service to their lord in return for his protection, shelter and a small strip of land to provide food for their families. Lords could buy and sell them, and they could not leave without permission.
A few peasants were free (not bound to the land), but most did not leave the local lord.

Landholding

The king kept about 20 per cent of land in England for himself, for hunting, farming and renting out. His land was known as **demesne**. Most of the rest (approximately 55 per cent) was run by barons, other nobles and knights. The remaining land was controlled by the Church, which made the Church very wealthy.

Key terms

Fief or feud – land held by a vassal in return for service to a lord.
Tenant-in-chief – someone who held their fiefs directly from the king.
Under-tenant – someone who held their fiefs from a tenant-in-chief.
Vassal – someone who held land from someone else in the feudal system.

Now try this

Describe **two** features of the relationship between vassals and their lords in the feudal hierarchy.

The nature of feudalism

Feudalism was based on **landholding** in return for paying homage and providing certain services. The nature of the system ensured that power firmly remained at the top of the feudal hierarchy.

Paying homage

All landholders had to pay **homage** to their lord by swearing an **oath of loyalty**. This oath was sworn in a public ceremony. Once it had been sworn, the landholder became the **vassal** of his lord and had to provide service to him. If a vassal broke his oath, he could be punished by **forfeiture** or even death.

Forfeiture

If a vassal failed to provide service to his lord, or committed a crime, his oath was considered broken, and his land was **forfeit** (the lord took it away). The land could then be granted to someone else as a reward for their loyalty. This helped maintain the feudal hierarchy and the king's power.

Vassals swearing allegiance to a medieval king in an act of homage.

Knight service

Knight service ensured that the king had an army to protect his kingdom. The amount of land held by a tenant-in-chief determined how many knights he owed the king. Some barons were allowed to pay **scutage** to the king instead of providing knights.

To find out about scutage, see page 9.

Labour service

This was the work that unfree peasants were expected to do on their lord's land. It helped ensure that enough food and other essential items, like wool for clothing, was produced to provide for everyone in the country.

Duties of knight service

Serving in the king's army for two months per year.

Guarding castles of their lord or the king for up to 40 days per year.

Raising money to pay the ransom of their lord if he was captured during battle.

Duties of labour service

'Boon-work' – working on the lord's land gathering in the harvest.

'Week-work' – working on the lord's land on certain days every week, doing jobs such as looking after animals, sowing crops, ploughing land.

Now try this

Explain how forfeiture helped maintain the feudal hierarchy.

Role and influence of the Church

The Church had enormous influence in medieval society. It owned land and property. Everyone was expected to go to Mass, and had to give the Church a percentage of their produce.

The importance of religion

Most people believed that God controlled everything and would decide whether they went to heaven or hell. Therefore pleasing God was vital, and the Church told people how to do this. The Church was an international organisation. Its structure, like the feudal system, was based on a hierarchy. The head was the pope, in Rome. As God's representative on Earth, the pope had huge authority, even over kings. He authorised the appointment of archbishops. Archbishops chose their bishops, but the king also had a say over who became an archbishop or bishop. This could cause conflict between kings and the pope. Another potential problem for kings was that clergy were more likely to be loyal to the pope than to the king if the pope and the king disagreed.

The head of the Church in England was the Archbishop of Canterbury. He was supported by the Archbishop of York.

Bishops were in charge of the priests and monks in their **diocese** (church district). Abbots were in charge of monasteries.

Pope (supreme leader)

Cardinals

Archbishops

Bishops and abbots

Priests

Deacons

The laity (people or church members who serve the hierarchy)

The structure of the Church.

Every parish (small area) had a priest who was responsible for his church and the people in his parish.

Influence of the Church

Spiritual
The clergy, who dedicated their lives to God, guided and taught people to live according to Church teachings – which included accepting the nature of feudalism, therefore helping to control society. Clergy performed daily services, including Mass, in all villages and towns in England. They also performed baptisms, marriages and funerals.

Economic
The Church was very wealthy: it earned money from rent and profits from agriculture on its land; people frequently donated money and land to the Church or left money in their wills; everyone paid a tithe (a tenth of their produce) to the Church every year.
As a major landholder, the Church had many vassals and employees. Therefore many people depended on the Church for their land, food and employment.
The Church was an important source of money for the king, as it paid taxes to him on the money earned from its land. The king relied on this income, which gave the Church influence over the king.

The Church in medieval society.

Political
As tenants-in-chief and under-tenants, members of the clergy provided knight service for the king.
Important churchmen, along with the barons, were leading members of government and advised the king.
Many clergy were well educated, and became clerks in important households, including the king's.
The king, like all Catholics, was under the authority of the pope, who could therefore influence the king's policies and actions.

Social
Priests and monks taught people to read and write, and some church buildings housed large collections of books.
Monasteries, nunneries and parish priests looked after the elderly, poor and sick.
Many churchmen played major roles in law courts and the Church kept collections of the laws.

Now try this

Explain how the Church was so wealthy and why this gave it power and influence in medieval England.

The nature of kingship

Kingship in medieval times was very different from the monarchy today. The king had immense power, but he also had responsibilities in the form of duties he was expected to perform.

Rights

In 1189, once the king of England was crowned at the **coronation**, he had almost unlimited rights to act as he wanted, because he had been chosen by God to be king. He could make laws, decide on foreign and domestic policy, raise an army, set taxes and mint coins. However, he was expected to fulfil certain duties in order to govern and protect his people.

Display

In order to maintain authority and keep his subjects under control, a medieval king needed to display his power and majesty by showing himself to his people. Rituals were an important part of this, but the king also regularly travelled around the country meeting barons, nobles and bishops. This practice is known as **itinerant kingship**.

Domestic duties

Duties expected of the king		How the king was to carry out this duty
Law-maker	To maintain justice and show mercy and fairness	The king was expected to consult with leading barons and churchmen in making laws to ensure they were fair. The king heard court cases himself and sent his own judges to settle other cases.
YES — Decision-maker	To govern in the interest of his people	The king was expected to govern fairly and make policy decisions that would benefit his people. He was expected to consult with leading barons and churchmen to help him do this.
Christian	To support and respect the Church	People believed the king had been chosen by God, and they expected him to behave like a good Christian and follow the advice of leading churchmen.
Protector	To defend the land and people from attack	The king was in charge of the army. He was expected to have the military strategy and skills to lead it effectively. Most kings led the army into battle themselves.

Rituals

Coronation

The king was crowned in the coronation ceremony at Westminster Abbey, in front of important nobles and churchmen. He was anointed with 'holy oil' to show that he was made king by God. The king had to take the coronation oath, where he swore to protect the Church and act with justice and mercy. The tenants-in-chief then swore homage to the king.

See page 2 to read about homage.

Crown-wearings

Three times a year, during religious festivals at Winchester (Easter), Gloucester (Christmas) and Westminster (Whitsun), the king took part in crown-wearing ceremonies which nobles were expected to attend. These took place in important cathedrals to enforce the message that the king had been chosen by God.

Now try this

Explain why rituals were important for a medieval king.

Richard I as king

On 3 September 1189, Richard I was crowned king of the Angevin Empire in a lavish ceremony. Richard took power peacefully and set about preparing his kingdom for his absence when he left on **crusade** three months later.

Richard I

Born: 1157

Nickname: Coeur de Lion (Lionheart)

Claim to the throne in 1189: eldest surviving son of Henry II and Eleanor of Aquitaine; experienced ruler; Duke of Aquitaine since 1172; a successful and proven military leader; favourite son of Eleanor (who held much power and influence)

Character and qualities: charismatic; brave; strong belief in chivalry; a great soldier; wrote music and poetry; arrogant; selfish; could be disloyal (he had fought against his father and brothers during his father's reign)

How power was secured

When Henry II died in 1189, Richard succeeded to the throne peacefully and successfully secured his power by:

- making peace with those who had fought against him while his father was alive

- appeasing those with other strong claims to the throne – he made his brother John, Count of Mortain (in Normandy), and his half-brother Geoffrey, Archbishop of York, but he also banned them from England for three years

- agreeing that William the Lion (king of Scotland) did not have to do homage to him (accepting Scotland as a separate country) in return for William abandoning claims to northern England

- putting able, loyal men, such as William Longchamp, in charge in his absence

- winning the support of many barons by restoring land to nobles who had been disinherited by Henry II, using patronage to reward powerful barons

- treating nobles and knights with courtesy and respect and inspiring loyalty with his charisma.

Death of Richard I

In March 1199, Richard was badly wounded while fighting in France. He died on 6 April. As he had no children, he had named John as his heir. However, his nephew Arthur, the son of John's older brother Geoffrey, claimed that he should be king, according to the principle of **primogeniture** (where the eldest son inherits). Following the rules of primogeniture, Arthur would inherit before John because Arthur was a son of an older brother.

Many people at the time and since regarded Richard I as a great warrior-king. He is often portrayed this way in paintings and statues.

Now try this

Explain Richard I's claim to the throne in 1189.

John as king

John's succession to the throne was not as smooth as Richard's had been. In England he established his authority quickly; elsewhere it took time for his power to be secured. Indeed, in some parts of the Angevin Empire, John never really secured power at all.

John

Born: 1167

Nickname: (earlier) Lackland; (later) Softsword

Claim to the throne in 1199: fourth and only surviving son of Henry II and Eleanor of Aquitaine; favourite son of Henry II; acknowledged by Richard I as his heir; his claim was supported by his mother

Character and qualities: intelligent; hard-working; experienced in warfare (though he lacked the generalship of Richard); had spent some time in England; 'trained' by his father to be king (though he lacked Henry's diplomatic skills); short tempered; could be cruel; suspicious and distrusting of others; could be disloyal

How power was secured

Leading English and Norman barons, and his mother, supported John's claim to the throne. Other key men in Anjou, Maine and Touraine supported John's nephew Arthur, Duke of Brittany (also known as Prince Arthur). John's biggest threat was Philip II of France, who supported Arthur's claim and invaded Normandy when he heard of Richard's death. However, John secured power through:

- acting quickly by being crowned king on 27 May (Richard died 6 April)
- showing his religious devotion by visiting Canterbury and Bury St Edmunds after his coronation, inspiring loyalty from his English subjects
- wisely leaving England to be run by men who had governed under Richard, while going to fight for his lands in France
- ensuring the north of England was protected from the threat of Scottish invasion by entrusting its protection to a powerful and loyal baron
- securing the support of the Count of Angouleme by marrying his daughter Isabelle, and persuading the Count of Anjou to switch sides
- driving back Philip II's forces and making peace in May 1200 at Le Goulet.

Peace lasted for two years and secured John's position as king, but only for a short time.

The Treaty of Le Goulet

- Philip recognised John as king of the Angevin Empire.
- John gave Philip some land in Normandy.
- Arthur remained Duke of Brittany but did homage to John for this.
- John agreed to do homage to Philip for his land in France and pay an enormous fine for the inheritance of this land.

The murder of Prince Arthur

John's army had captured Arthur at Mirebeau in August 1202. Like other captured nobles, Arthur was imprisoned in chains, which went against the chivalric code. There are different versions of what happened next, but Arthur disappeared. Whatever actually happened, John was blamed for his murder; some people even believed that John killed his nephew himself. The consequence of Arthur's disappearance was that many of John's supporters in France changed sides and supported Philip, eventually leading to John losing Normandy completely.

Turn to page 21 for more about Arthur's murder and the loss of Normandy.

Now try this

Explain why John found it more difficult to secure power than Richard when he took the throne.

England under Richard

During most of his ten-year reign (1189–99), Richard I was on crusade: he spent only six months in England. In his absence, England was ruled by **justiciars** (who heard law cases and had the authority of the king when he was not there) with varying degrees of success.

Timeline

1189 In December, Richard leaves England for France.

1191 John arrives in England, stirs up rebellions and seizes some castles. Longchamp is deposed in October and replaced by Walter of Coutances.

1193 John pays homage to Philip II. John seizes more castles in England, declares Richard dead and himself king. Hubert Walter becomes justiciar.

1198 Geoffrey Fitz Peter becomes justiciar.

1189 In July, Richard becomes king.

1190 Richard departs on crusade, appointing Longchamp as justiciar.

1192 Richard is captured.

1194 Richard returns to England, takes control, then leaves for France.

1199 Richard is killed in France.

William Longchamp

Longchamp was loyal to Richard but unpopular with many English barons because:

- he was Norman and they felt they knew English government better than him
- he had paid Richard to make him chancellor
- he replaced many sheriffs appointed by Richard with his own men
- they felt he was arrogant and didn't treat them with respect or consult them on important matters.

In October 1191, Longchamp was deposed after leading barons joined with Prince John in rebellion against him. Richard sent Walter of Coutances to become the new justiciar, but Prince John continued to cause problems.

Turn to pages 13–18 for details of Richard's crusade, his capture and ransom, and pages 19–21 for more about his time in France after 1194. You can find out more about rule in England on pages 9–12.

John's rebellions

In 1191, John arrived in England and encouraged the barons to rebel against Longchamp's rule. He set up his own court, hired sheriffs to collect taxes for him and seized control of several castles. In 1193, after hearing of Richard's capture, John attempted to seize the throne. He paid homage to Philip II of France for Richard's lands in France. He then returned to England, seized more castles and declared that Richard was dead and he was king. However, he didn't have many supporters. Coutances met with leading barons and they decided to believe that Richard was alive and to pay the ransom that was demanded. After Richard's release in 1194, John surrendered the castles and begged for mercy. Richard forgave his brother and named him his heir before he died.

Hubert Walter

Walter had worked for Henry II and was respected by most barons. He had also served Richard well on crusade and was made Archbishop of Canterbury in 1193. The barons appointed him justiciar in December 1193. Illness forced him to resign in 1198, when Geoffrey Fitz Peter took over the role.

England was well governed until 1199 because:

- Richard was often close by in Normandy and stayed in touch with Walter, authorising and approving his actions
- Walter and Richard had the support of the barons and consulted with them
- Walter made the justice system more effective by choosing four knights in each hundred (an area within a shire) to deal with justice in an area.

Now try this

Give **two** reasons why Richard ruled England well and **two** reasons why he ruled England badly.

England under John

During the years 1199–1204, John spent most of his time in France, trying to secure the Angevin lands. In his absence, England was ruled by justiciars. John spent the years 1204–16 ruling in England. He played a far greater role in running England than Richard had done.

1199–1204

When John became king and left for France, Fitz Peter continued as justiciar and Hubert Walter was appointed chancellor, showing how John kept most of Richard's main officials in place to rule in his absence. They are generally regarded as having done a good job. However, in 1204, John lost Normandy and returned to England, where he ruled for himself until his death in 1216. His rule of England became very unpopular and was seen at the time, and since, as oppressive.

For more about the loss of Normandy, turn to page 21.

Positive views of John

✓ John was more interested in governing England than many of his predecessors had been. He is described as hard-working and energetic.

✓ He paid great attention to detail and kept efficient records of day-to-day government that show how much work he did.

✓ Government records show that John could be generous and often gave donations to the poor.

Many descriptions and images of King John come from 13th-century chroniclers. They were monks and therefore had negative opinions about a man who had argued with the pope. They portray John as, at best, useless and, at worst, a tyrant. This image is from Matthew Paris' chronicle, c.1250–59, and depicts John with his crown falling off his head.

Reasons for John's unpopularity

1 As John did most of the governing himself and was almost continuously in the country after 1204, he was blamed when things went wrong. In the past, regents or government ministers had taken the blame for unpopular policies.

2 As time went on, he replaced his advisers with 'new men', many of whom were inexperienced in government and/or exploited their influence to gain large financial rewards. John relied on a small number of people, which meant he had few supporters.

3 The 'new men' took the place of wealthy English barons in advising the king, which annoyed and angered the barons. Unlike Richard, John did little to gain the support of the barons, who he seems to have distrusted.

4 The ways John raised money through taxes and fines to pay for (unsuccessful) wars caused hardship and annoyance. Many barons owed large debts due to John's increasing demands.

Go to page 25 for more about John and the barons.

5 John's dispute with the pope worried and angered some of his subjects, especially churchmen.

See page 22 for more about the dispute with the pope.

6 John took almost complete control over justice. Many saw him as applying the law to benefit himself, as only he heard cases in the royal court.

7 The suspected murder of Arthur, the cruel punishment of those who displeased John, as well as reports that John attempted to seduce many barons' wives, made him hated and feared.

Turn to page 6 to read about Arthur's role and his death.

Now try this

Give **three** reasons for the English barons' dislike of King John.

Use pages 25 and 26 as well as this one to help you answer this question.

Royal revenues

Richard and John needed to raise huge amounts of money: Richard needed to fund his crusade and pay his ransom, and both kings needed to pay for wars in France. They raised money from their English subjects by various means. Prices rose after 1200, which increased the need for money.

Royal demesne
The land held directly by the king raised money through the sale of crops and livestock. It also brought in rent from the towns and the countryside, and by **tallage** (land tax). Tallages were paid only by peasants and were greatly resented. Throughout his reign, John increased the amount paid by towns and cities.

Feudal incidents
These were charges the king could make his vassals pay for ransoming the king if he was captured, to knight the king's eldest son and pay for the king's eldest daughter's dowry. They also included forest fines, **wardship** (under-age children, called wards, who inherited land were looked after by the king until they came of age and had to pay for their land) and inheritance fines (known as reliefs). John greatly increased both forest fines and wardship fines, which made him a lot of money, but this fell heavily on the barons.

Court cases
All fees for a writ starting a court case were paid to the king, and both Richard and John raised funds this way. In addition, the possessions of any person convicted of a crime went to the king. During John's reign the crown also raised considerable funds in return for favourable judgements in court – this led to complaints that John sold justice.

How Richard I and John raised money

Selling offices
It was usual for positions, such as sheriff, to be bought. Both kings sold many positions. Richard raised vast amounts of money for his crusade this way in just a few months after becoming king in 1189. He then raised money in 1194 for war in France by charging men to retain the offices they had bought in 1189!

Scutage
This could be paid by tenants-in-chief instead of providing knight service to the king when the king demanded it. The king set the amount to be paid according to the amount of land held and therefore the number of knights due in knight service. Richard levied three scutages during his reign, and John levied 11. John also raised the amount due to be paid per knight. The money was used to hire professional soldiers during war.

Aids
Aids were taxes payable in exceptional circumstances. They were levied on income to pay Richard's ransom, and were demanded by John in 1207 in the form of his new type of tax on moveables and income to recover land in France.

For more about Richard's ransom, go to page 18.

Tax on moveables and income

A new tax introduced by John in 1207 on the income and moveables (goods or possessions) of every man at a rate of a **thirteenth** of the value. The penalty for failure to pay was seizure of moveables and imprisonment. It was very unpopular, and people went to great lengths to hide their goods. John didn't collect it again.

Role of sheriffs

Sheriffs had to collect all taxes due from the royal demesne. They were allowed to keep any money they collected above the required sum, so the office of sheriff could be a valuable one, which some sheriffs exploited. John increased the fixed sums demanded from each demesne, so sheriffs increased pressure on people taxed.

Now try this

List **three** similarities and **three** differences in the ways in which Richard and John raised money.

Rural medieval England

Medieval England was an agrarian rural society; very few people lived in towns. Most people lived in a manorial village and worked on the land. Life expectancy was low.

Animals, such as cows, sheep and pigs, were kept for food and to provide material for clothing. They grazed on common land around the village, and at night were put in barns or peasants' houses for safety. Peasants kept some animals for themselves. Wool was very profitable, and was traded in towns.

Land for farming was divided into strips. Each field grew a single crop: wheat, barley, rye or oats, depending on the soil. All work was done by **peasants**. Yields were often low, and poor harvests led to food shortages and sometimes starvation.

There were usually three large fields. One of these was left **fallow** (unfarmed) for a year or two to allow it to recover while crops were grown on the other two.

Work on the land was carried out from dawn until dusk and included hard work, such as clod-breaking. Peasant men, women and children were all expected to work on the land.

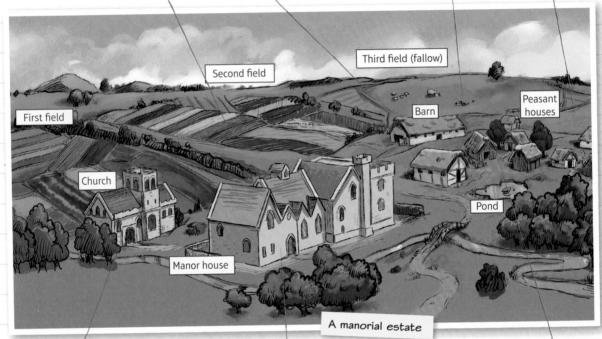

First field · Church · Manor house · Second field · Third field (fallow) · Barn · Peasant houses · Pond

A manorial estate

Religion and the Church were central to village life. Sunday was the peasants' only day off, and all were expected to go to church. Other holidays were around Christian festivals when people gathered to drink ale, and enjoy music and sports, such as wrestling.

The lord of the manor or his bailiff (manager) lived in the manor house. A lord was a baron, lesser noble or knight who held his land either directly from the king or as an under-tenant. He kept some land for himself and split the rest between the peasants who lived in the village.

Peasants lived in the village in one-room cruck houses with thatched roofs and wattle-and-daub walls. Unfree peasants were owned by the lord and had to work on his land. They were given strips of land to grow food to feed themselves and their families. Freemen paid rent for their land and sometimes worked on the lord's land, but were paid for this. All peasants had to pay the lord for using the village mill to grind their crops and for using his ovens to bake bread.

Look back at page 1 for the difference between free and unfree peasants.

Now try this

Describe **two** features of life for a medieval peasant.

Medieval towns

Although only a small percentage of England's population lived in towns, by 1189 towns were growing and new towns were developing due to increasing trade and prosperity. Towns were vital to the economy because they were centres of trade and an essential source of revenue for the king.

Life in towns and their role in the economy

All town dwellers were free and did not belong to a lord. This meant that men could choose their own employment. Some were tradesmen, such as blacksmiths, carpenters and bakers.

Others were merchants. Many townsmen were poor and worked as servants or labourers. Town dwellers usually had to pay tallage (land tax) to the king.

For a reminder about life in the villages of rural medieval England, go to page 10.

As in villages, the church was central to life in the towns, and all were expected to attend church on Sundays. People often went to the market afterwards.

As in villages, towns contained plots of land where people grew food for themselves and to sell. Local villagers and townspeople sold their surplus food and goods in the town's market.

Stone walls protected the town from thieves and attack, and gateways were controlled. Watchmen patrolled the town walls at night.

Some houses had shops at the front. Markets were often held on Sundays: traders paid rent for a table or stall. Larger towns paid the king for a licence to hold annual fairs, where goods and animals were sold, and people enjoyed drinking and sports. Villagers visited nearby towns to sell surplus produce and buy things they needed. Buying and selling took place in towns every day, and the king collected taxes on sales and purchases.

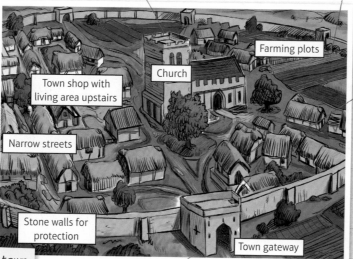

Farming plots

Church

Town shop with living area upstairs

Narrow streets

Stone walls for protection

Town gateway

A medieval town

Town authorities built and maintained roads and bridges. This helped both town dwellers and visitors, and so made trade easier. Tolls were paid to the king for using certain roads and bridges, and to enter towns through the gates.

Tradesmen

Tradesmen trained as apprentices to highly skilled master craftsmen. They were often members of a **guild** who had the right to trade in that town in return for members' fees and payment of taxes.

Merchants

Merchants sold food, raw materials and textiles in towns across England and even in Europe, especially the Low Countries. Some merchants were very wealthy. Customs duties on all imports and exports were paid to the king.

Read the question carefully. It's asking you about the **national** economy. What aspects of medieval town life helped the whole country?

Now try this

Describe **two** ways in which medieval towns were important to the national economy.

Jews in medieval England

By 1200, around 5000 Jews lived in England, mostly in large towns, such as London and York. They were an important part of England's economy, but lived in fear of attacks by Christians.

Legal status

👍 They were allowed to travel where they wanted, and were exempt from many travel tolls.

👍 They were allowed to trade and to inherit possessions.

👎 They, and their possessions, were essentially the property of the king. He could tax them whenever he wanted and however much he wanted.

👎 Local restrictions often barred them from some jobs. For example, they weren't allowed to join guilds, so couldn't find employment as skilled tradesmen.

Role in moneylending

Most Jews were moneylenders because:

• the Church didn't allow Christians to charge interest for lending money

• there were few other jobs, as Jews were barred from many occupations.

Jewish moneylenders were essential for England's economy as they provided loans for many barons and knights to buy land or positions. Some Jews such as Aaron of Lincoln, were incredibly wealthy.

Jews were the only non-Christians allowed to live in England. They did so under the protection of the king.

Anti-semitism

Prejudice, hatred and discrimination against Jews (anti-semitism) were growing throughout Europe in the late 12th century due to:

• accusations of being 'Christ-killers' and false rumours about Jews killing Christian children in rituals

• the Crusades, which highlighted religious differences and caused tensions

• the fact that many people owed Jews money and were jealous of their success in business.

Royal exploitation

Both Richard and John exploited Jews in England through taxation. Jews were forced to pay **tallages** at any time and, after 1194, the king could collect all debts owed to a Jew if he died without a will.

When Clifford's Tower in York Castle was attacked in 1190, some men killed their families before committing suicide. Others were killed when rioters broke their promise to leave them in peace.

The pogroms of 1189–90

A **pogrom** is a riot against a particular group of people. The pogroms of 1189—90 involved setting Jews' homes on fire, stealing their property and physically attacking and killing them. The pogroms were sparked by Christians who thought that the Jews offering a gift to Richard at his coronation in September 1189 was an insult to the new king. However, Richard was furious. He hanged the ringleaders and sent messages across England ordering people to leave Jews in peace. Despite this, the violence spread across the country, culminating in the massacre of Jews at York Castle.

Timeline

September 1189 There were anti-Jewish riots in London.

February 1190 There were anti-Jewish riots in King's Lynn and Norwich.

March 1190 Anti-Jewish riots in Stamford, Bury St Edmunds, Lincoln and York: 150 Jews took refuge from the riots at Clifford's Tower in York Castle, but the castle was attacked.

Now try this

Give **three** causes of the pogroms of 1189–90.

Causes of the Third Crusade

During the years 1189–94, Richard I was away from England on the Third Crusade. A **crusade** was a holy war. At this time, Christians and Muslims were fighting over control of the Holy Land.

The concept of crusade

By 1095, the Muslim **Seljuk Turks** had taken over the Holy Land, which had been part of the Christian Byzantine Empire. The pope claimed that Muslims were persecuting Christians who lived there, and preventing them from visiting Jerusalem. He appealed to Christians in Europe to go on crusade – travel to the Holy Land and win back control from the Seljuk Turks.

The **First Crusade** followed: thousands of European knights travelled to the Holy Land and captured land which became known as 'crusader states', including the city of Jerusalem. Many Muslims and Jews were killed.

The **Holy Land** is the area of the Middle East linked to Jesus Christ and includes parts of modern Israel, Jordan, Syria, Lebanon and the Palestinian territories.

Indulgences

Pope Urban II, and later Pope Gregory VIII, promised Christians who went on crusade a **full indulgence**. The Church often sold indulgences to people who were anxious to reduce **penance** (punishment) for their sins and their time in **purgatory** (where they believed they would go after death to be 'purified' before going to heaven). A full indulgence meant complete forgiveness for sins committed on Earth, and immediate admission to heaven after death.

Causes of the Third Crusade

1. In 1144, Muslim forces took back control of parts of Edessa. This led to the **Second Crusade** as Christian armies attempted to win back Edessa.

2. After 1150, Muslim groups began to unite. By 1184 the crusader states were totally surrounded by Muslim lands, and were weakened by quarrels between the Christian lords ruling them.

3. In July 1187, Saladin led Muslim forces in a great victory over the Christian army at the Battle of Hattin.

4. Saladin's forces attacked Jerusalem. By October 1187, Jerusalem was back under Muslim control.

5. People in Europe were shocked and horrified to hear that Jerusalem had been taken. On 29 October 1187, Pope Gregory VIII issued a papal bull (an official declaration) describing horrible attacks on Christians by Muslims and calling for a **Third Crusade** to take back Jerusalem. He offered a full indulgence to those who went on crusade.

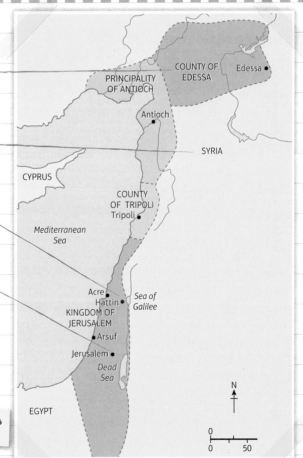

The four crusader states ruled by Christians by 1144. A Christian lord ruled each state.

Now try this

Define or describe the following: crusader states; papal bull; indulgence; Jerusalem. Then explain how each one is associated with the start of the Third Crusade.

The English crusading army

The Third Crusade was the first one to involve large numbers of crusaders from England. They went for a variety of reasons, and were largely supported by the population in England.

Who went on crusade

- Knights, including some from important noble families.
- Many knights' squires and other members of knights' military households.
- 8000 professional soldiers hired by Richard.
- A few important churchmen, including the Archbishop of Canterbury and Hubert Walter, Bishop of Salisbury.
- Many priests went to provide religious guidance and some fought as well.
- Civilians, including women, who worked as cooks, baggage carriers and nurses. Some were married to other crusaders.

People who vowed to go on crusade promised to 'take the cross'.

Attitudes in England to the crusaders

Most people supported their king's call for a crusade. It was seen as the highest duty that a king could perform, so many respected Richard for sticking to his promise (most medieval English kings promised to go on crusade, but only Richard ever did while he was king). Many were horrified by the news that Jerusalem was under Muslim control, and felt it was their Christian duty to support the crusade to recapture it.

There were some who resented the cost of the Third Crusade and worried about how lands would be managed while knights were away. A few had concerns about their king being absent from the country he ruled.

Why people went on crusade

Financial reasons

- Crusaders did not have to pay the crusading tax (known as the Saladin tithe).
- There would be opportunities to gain wealth and land in the Holy Land.
- Professional soldiers were paid for going on crusade.
- Crusaders' debts would be cancelled while they were away.

Religious reasons

- The pope promised all crusaders a full indulgence.
- Many priests persuaded people to go on crusade, often using tales of Muslim atrocities.
- Going on pilgrimage was common, and Jerusalem was the most sacred of all Christian sites.
- Many saw it as their religious duty to win back Christian control of the Holy Land, especially Jerusalem.

Other reasons

- To travel and go on an adventure.
- To win glory and respect for themselves and their family.
- To complete their knight service and fulfil their duty to their lord.
- To take revenge on the Muslims who had taken Jerusalem and killed Christians.

Now try this

Explain how going on crusade could benefit a knight financially.

Richard and the Third Crusade

Richard was the first of the princes to **take the cross** (agree to go on crusade) in the autumn of 1187. He left England for the Holy Land in December 1189, three months after his coronation.

Richard's motives for involvement

👍 He was religious and strongly believed it was his Christian duty.

👍 He was a great soldier with military experience, and believed this was his chance for honour and glory.

👍 Due to the wealth and size of his empire, he had the necessary resources.

👍 His great grandfather had been king of Jerusalem, so he had a family connection and desire to win it back.

Rivalry with Philip

Even before the crusade, a great rivalry was developing between Richard and Philip II of France. Philip had tried to take Angevin lands and stir up trouble between Richard, his brothers and his father, Henry II. With the smaller empire, Philip's resources were also smaller than Richard's. Finally, Philip had given Richard the Vexin (land in France) as the dowry for marrying his sister, but Richard never married her.

Richard's quarrel with Philip II

The routes taken by Richard I and Philip II to the Holy Land during the Third Crusade.

1 The third leader of the Third Crusade was Frederick I (Barbarossa) of the Holy Roman Empire. He drowned on the way to the Holy Land in **June 1190** and many of his men went home. This was a serious blow to the crusade, and increased the rivalry between Richard and Philip as both wanted to lead the crusade.

2 In **September 1190** Richard was greeted with a great ceremony on his arrival in Messina, Sicily. Philip, on the other hand, received a quiet reception and felt humiliated. After fighting erupted, Richard conquered Messina. Philip was annoyed. Richard gave him some of the money he made from the peace deal with Sicily's ruler.

3 Richard invaded and conquered Cyprus in **May 1191**, but this time, he refused to give Philip a share of its value. He sold the island for 100 000 gold coins and secured its grain supplies for his army.

4 In Cyprus, Richard married Berengaria of Navarre, going back on his agreement to marry Philip's sister.

5 Philip and Richard's quarrels also concerned strategy in the Holy Land. They disagreed over who should be king of Jerusalem (Richard wanted Guy de Lusignan and Philip, Conrad de Montferrat) and how much their professional soldiers should be paid (Richard paid more).

6 Despite winning at Acre in July, Philip returned home in **August 1191**. Annoyance with Richard was not Philip's only reason for leaving; he was unwell and had been told that the Count of Flanders had died, so he feared that France would be attacked in his absence.

Turn to page 16 to read about the victory at Acre.

Now try this

Give **three** reasons why Richard I and Philip II quarrelled on the Third Crusade.

Victories at Acre and Arsuf

Richard's victories at Acre and Arsuf enhanced his reputation as a great warrior and military leader that lasts to this day, though some of his actions were controversial.

The siege of Acre and Battle of Arsuf

1 Acre was the main port in the Kingdom of Jerusalem and therefore an important supply route to the town of Jerusalem. It had been under siege by crusaders since 1189.

Philip's forces reached the town in January 1191 and joined the siege. As Richard sailed towards Acre in June, his forces managed to sink enemy ships. Arriving at Acre on 8 June, his forces joined the attack on the city walls.

2 The siege of Acre

3 The walls were eventually breached by catapults and Philip's miners who had tunnelled under them. On 12 July 1191, only around a month after Richard's arrival, Saladin's forces surrendered Acre.

4 After Philip returned to France, Richard negotiated with Saladin. He agreed to release Muslim soldiers if Saladin paid 200 000 gold coins, released Christian prisoners and handed over siege weapons and the True Cross (believed to be the fragments from the cross on which Jesus died, which Saladin captured in 1187), but Saladin did not do any of this.

5 Richard believed Saladin was playing for time. On 20 August, Richard's men took 2700 Muslim prisoners to a spot within sight of Saladin's camp and executed them.

7 The crusaders' fleet also supplied the troops with water, food and a place to rest – essential in the heat and as local crops were destroyed by Saladin's forces. Despite frequent attacks by Saladin's skilled horsemen, under Richard's command the crusaders held their formation and Saladin realised his forces would have to face them in battle to stop them reaching Jaffa.

6 On 25 August, the crusader army left Acre and began the tough march to Jaffa on the way to Jerusalem. This march shows Richard's tactical expertise: his forces marched close to the sea, so that one flank was protected by the fleet and the other by archers and infantry (foot soldiers).

9 Richard I at the Battle of Arsuf

8 On 7 September 1191, Saladin's 30 000-strong army attacked the crusaders on the plain of Arsuf.

10 At a crucial moment in the battle, Richard courageously led his knights on a charge at Saladin's men. After an intense struggle, Saladin's army fled and the crusader army marched on to Jaffa.

Now try this

Give **two** examples of his actions at Acre, the march to Jaffa or the Battle of Arsuf that show Richard I was a great military leader.

Failure to recapture Jerusalem

Twice the crusaders marched to Jerusalem, but on both occasions they retreated. Richard I left the Holy Land without returning Jerusalem to Christian control as he had hoped.

First march on Jerusalem

After rebuilding Jaffa's defences Richard wanted to go to Ascalon, but he reluctantly agreed with other crusade leaders to march to Jerusalem. Progress was slow due to terrible weather. Mud and rain destroyed food, clothes and weapons. Progress was impossible, so Richard led the crusaders to Ascalon.

Second march on Jerusalem

By June the weather had improved and the crusaders marched to Beit Nuba in days rather than months. However, it was hot and the crusaders worried about lack of water, especially as Saladin had poisoned the wells around Jerusalem. After great debate, Richard decided to retreat again.

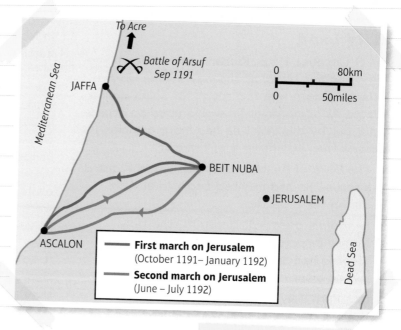

The marches to Jerusalem

Reasons for not attacking Jerusalem

- Leaving the coast left supply lines vulnerable to attack – they could be cut off from food and water supplies.
- Leaving the coast also meant they could be surrounded by Muslim forces and attacked from all sides without being able to retreat.
- Lack of troops to successfully besiege Jerusalem, which had strong defences, including fortresses and a wall.
- Lack of resources (people and money) to hold the city if they did win it.

Saving Jaffa

Once most crusaders had retreated to Ascalon for the second time, Saladin's troops tried to retake Jaffa. The leaders at Jaffa were about to surrender when Richard led a surprise attack to save the town. Saladin's army regrouped and attacked again, but again Richard successfully defended the city. Richard's bravery and skill during the battles were reported by many sources. The leaders of both sides decided to stop fighting at this point.

Reasons for the Treaty of Jaffa

Richard and Saladin stopped fighting and negotiated the Treaty:

- Richard had heard that his land was at risk from Philip II and John.
- Saladin was ill and was quickly running out of money to pay for war.

Turn to page 7 to read about John's rebellions.

The Treaty of Jaffa

- ✓ Muslims retained Jerusalem.
- ✓ Christians retained the coastline between Acre and Jaffa.
- ✓ Christian pilgrims could visit sacred sites in Jerusalem in safety.
- ✓ There would be no fighting for three years.

Now try this

Explain why Richard decided not to launch an attack on Jerusalem during the Third Crusade.

Richard's return and capture

Richard was captured while trying to return from the crusade, and the vast sum of money demanded for his ransom placed a huge burden on England.

Richard's return from the Holy Land

On 9 October 1192, Richard set sail for home. He could not travel all the way by sea, as the Atlantic Ocean was too rough for ships during winter. At some point he would need to cross land, but by this point he had more enemies in Europe than just Philip II of France:

- The Duke of Austria, Leopold, hated Richard because he had insulted Leopold at Acre during the crusade.

- Leopold's overlord, Henry VI, the Holy Roman Emperor, resented the fact that Richard had supported Henry's rival to the throne after Frederick I drowned in 1190.

- Northern Italy was ruled by a cousin of Conrad of Montferrat, who Richard had stopped becoming king of Jerusalem. There were also rumours that Richard was behind Conrad's murder in 1192.

Richard's capture

In November, Richard was shipwrecked off the northern Adriatic coast. He now had to cross enemy territory to get home. He and his few companions disguised themselves, but around Christmas he was recognised and arrested in Vienna by Duke Leopold's men. Leopold was delighted, as was Henry VI (who was handed Richard in February), even though the pope excommunicated both of them (officially excluded them from the Church), as crusaders were supposed to be able to travel freely across Europe. Henry wrote to Philip II and they, with Leopold, agreed the ransom figure. It was huge because Richard was so important. Henry and Leopold wanted as much money as they could get while Philip wanted the ransom to be high because he knew it would take time to raise such a huge sum, giving him time to capture some of Richard's land in France.

Turn to page 23 for more about the significance of excommunication.

The burden of the ransom on England

Henry VI, Holy Roman Emperor

demands the sum of

100 000 marks (£60 000)

for the release of

Richard,

King of England, Duke of Normandy, Count of Anjou, Duke of Aquitaine and Count of Poitou

Turn to page 7 for more on what was happening in England at this time.

John did not want to pay the ransom for his brother. However, leading English nobles wanted Richard back. They were supported by Richard's mother, Eleanor of Aquitaine, who took charge of collecting the ransom for him. It took six months to raise the massive sum by various means. Richard was released on 4 February 1194, after over a year in captivity.

 25 per cent aid was charged (a tax on income and moveables).

 Land tax on all tenants-in-chief and under-tenants.

 Tallage of £3375 on Jews.

 Gold and silver plate from churches in England.

 £1350 from the king of Scotland.

 A year's wool from Cistercian monks.

Now try this

Explain **three** ways money was raised to pay Richard's ransom.

Competing aims in Normandy

First Richard I and then John competed against Philip II of France for control of Normandy. For Philip, gaining control of Normandy would be an essential step towards his ultimate aim of controlling all of France. For Richard and John, Normandy was at the very heart of the Angevin Empire and therefore essential in keeping the empire together.

Why was Normandy important?

For Richard/John	For Philip	For all
It was the closest Angevin land in France to England, so provided a gateway to other regions. Also, losing it to Philip would increase the risk of him invading England.	Normandy, particularly the Vexin, was close to Paris, so whoever held the kingdom could threaten the French king's lands.	Normandy was very wealthy, with fertile farmland producing important crops and animal fodder.
Many leading English barons also held land in Normandy. If Richard or John lost Normandy it would reduce the barons' confidence in the king's ability to rule England.	Gaining control of Normandy would give Philip several options for winning more land, by invading either England or other Angevin lands in France.	Norman towns were wealthy and traded a lot with England – Philip wanted to gain this trade, while Richard/John didn't want to lose it.

The situation in 1194

When Richard returned after his imprisonment he secured England before setting sail for Normandy. His aim was to defend his territory in France and regain land already lost to Philip.

⬇

His rule of Normandy was hanging by a thread.

- As well as John, some important Norman barons had switched sides and now supported Philip.
- Philip (with John's help) had taken control of most of western Normandy, including the Vexin region.
- Philip now controlled strategically important castles, such as Gisors.
- Philip also controlled two harbours, so he could attack by sea as well as land.
- Philip's army was not far from Normandy's capital, Rouen.

⬇

Upon Richard's return to England, John threw himself on his brother's mercy and Richard forgave him, meaning that he only had one enemy to fight as well as gaining John's (and his army's) support. That still left Philip with the ascendancy, however.

Why did Richard achieve his aims?

In 1194, Richard's main aims in Normandy were to defend the land he held and regain land lost to Philip during his captivity. In January 1199, Philip agreed that everything he had captured would go back to Richard, except Gisors. Richard had successfully achieved his aims due to various factors.

Military skill: Richard's army, and John's, successfully laid siege to many castles, defended their own castles and won several battles.

Bribery: Richard successfully bribed many nobles to switch sides and support him instead of Philip, thereby taking back control of territory and bringing more knights under his control.

Forging alliances: Richard made important alliances with leaders, such as the counts of Toulouse, Flanders and Boulogne, meaning Philip was surrounded by enemies.

The building of Chateau Gaillard was another factor in Richard's success. Turn to page 20 to read why.

Now try this

Give **three** reasons why Normandy was important to all three kings (Richard I, John and Philip II).

Chateau Gaillard

As part of his plan to achieve his aims in Normandy, Richard built a magnificent castle – Chateau Gaillard. It was regarded as having the finest defences in Europe, but the cost was enormous.

Location

Built on the River Seine, on the border of Normandy and overlooking the Vexin, the castle defended the main route from Paris to Rouen. It was close enough to Rouen for men and supplies to reach it easily by road, but its location on the river also meant that ships could reach it fairly easily from England. As well as being an excellent defensive structure, it also provided a good base from which to attack castles in the Vexin.

Structure

Richard and his advisers used their great experience of the crusader castles in the Holy Land in the design, and the castle was the pinnacle of medieval engineering. Around the central great tower were several thick walls with huge towers to defend them. Many of the walls were curved, meaning there were no weak corner points for catapult stones to strike.

The ruins of Chateau Gaillard still show its rounded walls. Its position on a steep hill overlooking a river also made it difficult to attack.

Cost and time

The castle cost the vast sum of £12 000, nearly twice what Richard had spent on castles in England. It took just two years to build, although some historians think it was never completed.

Site

The castle was sited on a narrow plateau around 600 feet long and 200 feet wide, surrounded by deep ravines leading to the river. The steep slopes around the castle made attack difficult, as well as making it nearly impossible to mine under the walls.

The importance of Chateau Gaillard

- It defended Normandy's capital, Rouen, and therefore Normandy as a whole, from French attack.
- It was also a good base from which to attack Philip II's lands, and Richard had almost totally retaken the Vexin by January 1199.

- It provided a magnificent palace where Angevin kings could demonstrate their wealth and power to allies and enemies.
- Its huge cost put additional strain on the finances of England, but most barons accepted that it was worth it if the castle successfully defended Normandy.

Now try this

Explain why Richard built Chateau Gaillard.

John's loss of Normandy

When Richard died in April 1199, John succeeded him, ruling an empire nearly as large as when Richard had inherited the throne in 1189. Just five years later, John had lost Normandy.

See page 6 for more information about events before war restarted in 1202.

Timeline

August 1202 Arthur's forces besiege Mirebeau, while Eleanor of Aquitaine is trapped inside. John and his army spectacularly relieve the siege, rescue his mother and capture Arthur and other nobles.

Summer 1203 Philip takes Anjou and Maine before entering Normandy from the south and capturing important castles, including Vaudreuil, which surrender without a fight.

December 1203 John returns to England.

24 June 1204 Rouen surrenders to Philip. Normandy is entirely under Philip's control.

Easter 1202 John refuses to attend Philip II's court to answer charges of injustice against Hugh de Lusignan after marrying Isabelle of Angouleme. Philip declares John's continental lands forfeit.

Easter 1203 Arthur disappears. Believing John murdered his nephew, many barons who had supported John switch sides to Philip.

September 1203 Philip besieges Chateau Gaillard.

6 March 1204 Philip takes Chateau Gaillard.

Why war restarted

Isabelle of Angouleme had been promised in marriage to Hugh de Lusignan. When John married her to secure some of his lands in France he did not offer the Lusignans compensation. Hugh appealed for help to Philip II, John's overlord who he had paid homage to. John refused to attend Philip's court after he had been summoned. This gave Philip the opportunity to forfeit John's land in France and launch an attack. He claimed Normandy for himself and declared Arthur lord of all of John's other lands in France. John quickly left England with an army to defend his French lands.

The fall of Chateau Gaillard

John initially sent forces to attack the French when they reached Chateau Gaillard in September 1203, but they were unsuccessful. Rather than send more troops, John returned to England in December to try to persuade more barons and knights to help him. After an impressive defence the castle fell to Philip's siege after six months. The strength of the castle is shown by the fact it took Philip only three months to conquer the rest of Normandy.

John lost key allies: John's treatment of Arthur and other noble prisoners caused many powerful nobles in both England and France to switch sides.

English barons: After years of war, English barons were reluctant to fight in or finance another war.

Lack of money: John could not afford to hire more professional soldiers or bribe nobles in France to remain his allies (as Richard had done).

Philip's skill and ambition: Philip II was a good military leader and skilled diplomat who could win people to his side.

Why John lost Normandy

John's diplomatic mistakes: Paying homage to Philip in 1200 meant Philip could legally declare John's lands forfeit in 1202. If John had compensated Hugh de Lusignan for the loss of Isabelle of Angouleme, Lusignan would probably not have gone to Philip in the first place.

To read about John's oath to Philip, and his marriage to Isabelle, turn to page 6.

John's military mistakes: Many people, both at the time and since, have criticised John for leaving Normandy when he did – it looked as though he had abandoned his soldiers. He also failed to send more troops and resources to relieve Chateau Gaillard – keeping control of this was vital.

Now try this

Give **two** reasons why the loss of Normandy was John's own fault and **two** reasons why it wasn't.

John vs the papacy: causes

John was not the first king to quarrel with a pope, but his dispute with the papacy is important because it is one of the reasons why John gained a reputation as a poor king.

Causes of the dispute

As well as being England's leading churchman, the archbishop of Canterbury was also one of the king's main advisers. Hubert Walter, who had served Richard and then John well, died in July 1205. The dispute between King John and Pope Innocent III began because they disagreed over who should be the new archbishop.

John decided that John de Gray, Bishop of Norwich, should get the job; he told the monks of Canterbury his choice.

↓

The monks of Canterbury disagreed. They voted for one of their own men, a monk called Reginald.

↓

Both choices were sent to Pope Innocent, who, after summing up both candidates, decided on another man: Stephen Langton.

↓

John was angry and refused to accept Langton as archbishop.

↓

The pope made Langton archbishop anyway.

↓

John would not allow Langton into England. He expelled the monks from Canterbury and seized land from Italian clergy in England (because the pope is based in Rome).

↓

The pope placed England under an Interdict.

To read more about the Interdict, turn to page 23.

Remember that, in medieval society, the Church was immensely powerful. The pope, based in Rome, was its supreme leader - God's representative on Earth. The Church influenced all aspects of life: spiritual, political, social and economic. The king relied on income from taxes paid by the Church, and this gave the Church influence over the king.

Why disagree over Stephen Langton?

I should be able to choose my own archbishop of Canterbury as other kings have before me. I rule England, not the pope, it's unacceptable for one of my main advisers not to be chosen by me. I don't know or trust Stephen Langton; he's been working in Paris with my enemy Philip II.

I am God's representative on Earth. Kings should do what I tell them. Stephen Langton is English, he was born in Lincoln. I've studied and spent time with him. He's a very holy man and a good choice for archbishop.

Innocent III became pope in 1198 at the relatively young age of 37. He was determined to assert his authority over all kings in Europe. Rome made attempts to stop European monarchs making religious appointments, exemplified by Innocent's choice of Langton for archbishop of Canterbury.

Now try this

Explain why King John did not want Stephen Langton to become archbishop of Canterbury.

 Be sure to consider all reasons – not just John's objections to Langton.

The Interdict

As John continued to defy the pope and refused to accept Stephen Langton as archbishop of Canterbury, the pope placed England under an **Interdict** from March 1208 until July 1213.

Consequences of the Interdict

The Interdict meant that people in England were prevented from receiving most of the Christian sacraments. In practice, this meant that:

- the dying were not allowed to receive Mass and the sick could not be anointed
- marriages couldn't take place in church
- Christian burial was forbidden, so people had to be buried in woods or on common ground without a priest conducting the service
- baptisms were only allowed behind locked doors in the church
- religious services could not take place in a church.

Do not enter until Interdict is lifted.

The pope did relent slightly from 1209, so the clergy and monks and nuns could receive Mass behind church doors. The dying were also allowed to receive Mass.

The Interdict meant that lay people (ordinary Christians rather than priests or monks) were not allowed inside churches. The only exception to this was children, who were allowed in to be baptised.

The impact of the Interdict on everyday life

People were no doubt affected by the Interdict, but probably far less than the pope had intended.

- Priests still held services outside the church, sometimes in the churchyard.
- In some areas clergy ignored the Interdict and carried on as before.
- Most religious life, such as praying, fasting, celebrating festivals and going on pilgrimage, continued as it had always done.
- Lack of Christian burials were possibly the most worrying thing for many people, as they feared the souls of their dead loved ones would not go to heaven.

Most people in England seem to have sided with John rather than the pope at this stage. Some bishops left the country, but many clergy supported John, as did most nobles and barons.

John's response to the Interdict

John confiscated the property of any clergy who opposed him and kept any profit from this for himself. Clergy who wanted their property back had to pay a great deal of money for it. Some monks and their mistresses were arrested and only released on payment of a large fine. Therefore John profited a great deal financially from the Interdict.

John's excommunication

On 8 November 1209, the pope **excommunicated** John. This meant that John was excluded from all sacraments and Church services, and would go to hell when he died. It also meant that according to the Church, his subjects no longer had to obey him. Effectively, they had to choose between the Church and the king. Most chose the king, but some resented him for putting them in that situation. John responded to excommunication by seizing even more Church property and possessions.

Now try this

Explain what is meant by the terms 'interdict' and 'excommunication'.

John vs the papacy: reconciliation

In May 1213 John agreed to the pope's peace terms and even agreed to become his vassal. This may be seen as a humiliation for John, but it was actually a very clever move.

Look back at page 1 for what being a vassal involved.

Reasons for John's change of heart

In 1212, John had defeated a plot against him led by barons in England, but by 1213 he still lacked allies both in England and elsewhere in Europe. By reconciling with Innocent III, John would have the papacy as the most powerful ally of all.

Turn to page 26 for more on the plot of 1212.

By 1213, England was on the brink of invasion by Philip II's forces, led by Philip's eldest son, Prince Louis. Philip could claim this was a crusade with the pope's blessing, unless John and the pope were reconciled. John backed down to avoid an alliance between Innocent III and Philip.

John presents his crown to the pope's legate (representative), indicating his submission to the pope.

The terms of the reconciliation

John began negotiations with Innocent III in early 1213. Innocent said he would not reconcile unless John agreed to the following:

1 Stephen Langton to be allowed to take up office as Archbishop of Canterbury.

2 All clergy exiled from England to be allowed to return and their property given back to them.

3 Compensation to be paid to the pope.

John agreed to these terms, but went even further:

4 King of England and Lord of Ireland to hold his kingdoms from his overlord, the pope (so England would become a fief of Rome).

5 King of England to pay the pope 1000 marks per year.

The significance of the reconciliation

Innocent III was delighted with the terms of the reconciliation agreed by John. It appeared that he was victorious and had succeeded in asserting his authority over the king of England and Ireland, as John had become his vassal and held his kingdoms as fiefs from the pope.

For John, the reconciliation had effectively placed him, and England, under the pope's protection.

- This prevented Philip II's forces from invading England in 1213: attacking John's kingdom was now also an attack on the pope.
- It gave John and England an important ally against any future attack or invasion.
- It also gave John an extremely powerful ally to help with other problems that might arise in his kingdom – this would prove very useful in 1215.

The pope went on to support John after Magna Carta.

Revise the Magna Carta on page 28.

Now try this

Explain why the reconciliation between the pope and King John benefited them both.

Financial burdens

Between losing Normandy in 1204 and failing to regain it in 1214, King John's relations with the barons in England got steadily worse. The barons struggled with the financial burdens John placed on them and the arrogant way in which he exercised his power.

Growing financial impositions

To raise the vast sums of money needed to regain lands lost in France, John put the barons under enormous financial pressure with a variety of taxes and fines. Many went into debt, which angered many people as John spent large sums on clothing and jewels.

Scutage was raised 11 times in this period, almost annually (in contrast with the three times it was levied by Richard). The scutage in 1214 was the largest ever raised.

The amount charged in **wardship** fines increased by 300%.

Turn to page 9 for more about scutage and wardship, and the ways John raised money.

Fines for **inheriting** feudal land rose to four times what had previously been charged.

John started to lose the support of the barons.

Marriage fines were more frequently charged on barons who married without permission from the king.

Widows were fined if they did not agree to marry who John wanted. They were also fined if they wanted to inherit their husband's land but not remarry.

The 1207 **thirteenth** tax (on goods and income) also fell heavily on the barons.

See page 9 for more about the 1207 thirteenth tax.

Punishment for non-payment of fines

Another source of annoyance for the barons was the way they were pursued for money they owed. John and his favourites pressured barons to pay debts within a fixed period. If they did not do so, the king seized their lands and other possessions, and sometimes took their relatives hostage. This tactic was used as leverage far more frequently than before.

Financial problems

Not all of John's problems were his own fault:

- ✓ financing Richard's crusade and ransom, and Richard and John's wars in France, had left many people short of money
- ✓ losing Normandy in 1204 meant no more income from its land and tenants
- ✓ inflation (a rise in prices) meant that money was worth less than before.

Use of arbitrary power

John took almost total control of justice, and many barons resented how he seemed to manipulate the law to benefit himself. Between 1209 and 1214, only judges approved and directed by John were allowed to hear legal cases. John was accused of selling justice, as those who gave him money or goods won their cases. What happened to William de Braose is a clear example of the financial pressure John placed on barons and his use of arbitrary power in dealing with people however he wanted.

William de Braose

- ✓ One of John's leading barons, he held land in England, Wales and Ireland.
- ✓ William had agreed to pay John for this land, but by 1207 had only paid a little.
- ✓ In 1208, John took his land in England and Wales. William fled to Ireland.
- ✓ In 1210, when John went to Ireland, William fled to France, but his wife and eldest son were captured.
- ✓ John put them in prison, where many historians believe they starved to death.

Now try this

You could also use pages 8, 9 and 26 to help you answer this question.

Explain **three** ways in which King John angered the barons between 1204 and 1214.

The 1212 plot and failure in Normandy

In 1212 some of the barons were so angry with John that they plotted to remove him and choose someone else as king. John acted swiftly to defeat the barons, but discontent would increase again: in 1214, after raising huge amounts of money from them, John failed to regain Normandy.

The plot of 1212

In the summer of 1212, John was preparing to invade Wales to win back control of areas controlled by the Welsh prince, Llywelyn, when he heard of a plot to kill him. The plot was led by two powerful barons who were in league with Llywelyn: Eustace de Vesci and Robert Fitz Walter.

John acted swiftly; instead of invading Wales, he marched his army north to reassert control and prevent rebellion. De Vesci fled to Scotland and Fitz Walter to France. Consequences of the plot included:

- John making some concessions, including relaxing some tax demands
- John reconciling with the pope.

Revise John's reconciliation with the pope on page 24.

The 1212 plotters

Eustace de Vesci held large amounts of land in northern England. He borrowed money from Jewish moneylenders to pay taxes and fines to John. He accused John of trying to seduce his wife.

Robert Fitz Walter held land throughout England. He owed John large amounts of money, was annoyed with John for not supporting his claim to Hereford Castle, and accused John of trying to seduce his daughter.

In 1211, **Llywelyn** led a rebellion in Wales and seized some land. John attacked and forced Llywelyn into a peace settlement, including surrendering his son as John's hostage. Llywelyn continued to defy John and agreed to work with Philip II of France, as well as being involved in the 1212 plot.

Failure in France

John left for France in February 1214, well prepared with a large, experienced army mostly paid for by the barons through scutage (the largest ever raised), and feudal taxes and fines. John had powerful allies in Otto IV (the Holy Roman Emperor) and the counts of Boulogne, Flanders and Holland, who all wanted to defeat Philip II of France. They planned to attack from both the north and the south. John's campaign in the south ended in failure, but the most important battle took place in the north at Bouvines on 27 July 1214. It was close, but John's allies lost, and his hope of regaining Normandy had gone forever.

Many historians believe that defeat at the Battle of Bouvines, combined with the immense scutage levied to pay for the French campaign, led directly to baronial rebellion and Magna Carta.

The impact of the failure to regain Normandy in 1214

- 👎 John returned to England defeated and discredited, his war chest of some £130 000 wasted.
- 👎 The barons who had financed the campaign were very angry with him. It added to John's financial problems – he had spent vast sums on the campaign and permanently lost revenue from Normandy.
- 👎 John's reputation as a 'softsword' (a nickname based on military weakness) was cemented, which added to him being seen as a poor king.
- 👎 Philip II's victory at Bouvines in 1214 meant that he had defeated both the Angevins and the Holy Roman Emperor, making France the most powerful nation in Europe.

Now try this

Explain why failing to regain Normandy in 1214 caused such anger among the barons towards King John.

The rebellion of 1215

John returned to England after losing Normandy in October 1214. Soon, some of the barons began to make demands on him. This led to the rebellion of 1215, which ended with Magna Carta.

Timeline

November 1214 Some of the angry barons met at Bury St Edmunds. They swore that if John refused to accept the terms of Henry I's coronation charter, they would start a rebellion.

Henry I's charter (issued at his coronation in 1100) promised that the king would restore good government and get rid of 'evil customs'.

John played for time. He sent William Marshal and Stephen Langton to negotiate, but they were not allowed to agree to anything – this is why the barons moved to violent rebellion.

January 1215 John agreed to meet the rebel barons in London. He refused their demands but agreed to meet them again in April.

March 1215 John 'took the cross' to gain the pope's support.

Promising to go on crusade ensured John had the protection of the Church and the pope's support.

April 1215 The rebel barons mustered an army in Northampton and sent another set of demands (there is no record of what these were) which John refused. Meanwhile, John received letters of support from the pope.

5 May 1215 Rebel barons broke their oath of fealty to John and marched on Northampton led by Fitz Walter. They failed to take the town but started marching to London, and took control of Norfolk, Suffolk and Lincoln.

The castles at Northampton and Lincoln were well defended by royal forces so weren't taken by the rebels.

Winning East Anglia and the important town of Lincoln gave the rebel army momentum.

12 May 1215 Lands of the 39 rebel barons were seized by John.

17 May 1215 Rebel barons gained control of London and its financial resources.

27 May 1215 Negotiations between king and barons began.

Losing London was a major blow to John, as he lost revenue that would have helped quash the rebellion. It forced him into negotiations which led to Magna Carta.

15 June 1215 John sealed Magna Carta.

The rebel barons

By June 1215, around 39 barons out of 165 rebelled against John. Most, but not all, were from the north. They included Eustace de Vesci and were led by Robert Fitz Walter.

See page 26 for more information about the barons' plot against John in 1212.

A similar number of barons supported John, including William Marshal. Most refused to take sides, waiting to see what happened.

King John sealing Magna Carta. It was almost immediately annulled by Pope Innocent III.

Now try this

What were the key moments of the 1215 rebellion that led to King John agreeing to Magna Carta?

Runnymede

The rebel barons were outnumbered and did not want a war unless it was absolutely unavoidable – they wanted to limit the king's power over them. The final agreement, Magna Carta, was based on addressing the barons' grievances with John. It was sealed at Runnymede, Surrey, on 15 June 1215.

Motives of the barons

John's demands for higher and more frequent tax and aid had put many barons in debt.

Although the king had the right to feudal fines, such as inheritance and wardship, John had demanded much more than was considered fair.

Money

Few barons played their traditional role of advising the king and being consulted.

John had almost total control of the legal system and was accused of using arbitrary power to benefit himself.

Justice

Power

John relied on a small number of 'new men' for advice, and he rewarded these men rather than the barons.

Punishments for those who had committed crimes were often considered unfair. Barons also accused John of selling justice.

Behaviour

Some barons accused John of seducing or trying to seduce their wives and daughters.

John had treated some people very cruelly, such as the de Braose family.

John had made barons' widows marry men of his choice. If they refused they had to pay large fines.

Main provisions of Magna Carta

1. The English Church shall be free. Elections of churchmen will be decided by the Church alone.
2. Inheritance fines are set at £100.
3. Wards shall not have to pay a fine to receive their inheritance when they come of age.
7. When her husband dies, a widow shall have her inheritance at once. She will not pay anything for it.
8. Widows shall not be forced to marry but cannot marry without the consent of their lord.
12. Scutage and aid may only be raised with the agreement of the barons.
20. For freemen, fines shall only be levied in proportion to the seriousness of the crime. They should not be so great as to deprive a freeman of his livelihood.
21. Barons shall only be fined after a trial and the fine should be proportionate to the crime.
39. No freeman can be arrested, imprisoned or have his lands confiscated without a fair trial by his peers.
40. The king shall not sell justice or delay or deny it to anyone.
51. Any man who has had his lands confiscated without trial shall have them returned.
61. A council of 25 barons, chosen by the barons, will advise the king and make sure he keeps to the charter. If the king refuses, he or his family cannot be attacked but his possessions and lands can be taken.

Now try this

'Magna Carta only addressed the barons' own wishes.' Give **two** reasons for and **two** reasons against this statement.

The outbreak of war

Magna Carta was in force for just over two months; by October the country was in the grip of a civil war known as the First Barons' War.

The build-up to war

John agreed to Magna Carta as another delaying tactic. Shortly after sealing it, he wrote to the pope, appealing for help. On 24 August, Innocent III issued a papal bull which declared Magna Carta void because John had been forced into it, and pledged to excommunicate anyone who tried to enforce it. John then renounced Magna Carta.

The rebel barons decided there was no point trying to negotiate with John again. Instead, they invited Prince Louis, son of Philip II of France, to become king of England. They also promised land to King Alexander II of Scotland if he sent forces to help them.

The taking of Rochester

Rochester Castle was important strategically, as it was on the route from Dover to London and would be needed to defend or attack the capital. The rebels took control of it in October 1215. John arrived shortly after, took control of the town and laid siege to the castle.

The rebels held out for seven weeks before surrendering to John on 30 November. This was the start of a revival of John's fortunes. He marched north and recovered land taken by Alexander II, including Berwick Castle. By March 1216, only London still held out against John.

The siege of Rochester Castle

The bridges were destroyed, preventing supplies reaching the castle.

Five siege machines pounded the high and very thick castle walls with stones.

Miners dug under the walls of the castle. One of the towers collapsed.

Rochester Castle, where the rebels surrendered.

The invasion of Prince Louis

Prince Louis landed in Kent on 21 May with an army of 1200 knights. John retreated as he did not want to face Louis in battle. Louis quickly took most of Kent, including Rochester Castle. He arrived in London to a hero's welcome.

The tide had started to turn the rebels' way:

- By the end of July, rebel forces had retaken control of Essex, Norfolk and Suffolk. They also took control of Yorkshire and Lincolnshire. In August, Alexander II captured Carlisle.

- More barons joined the rebels. Some, including the Earl of Salisbury, switched sides. About two-thirds of barons now supported the rebels.

- On 15 October, John died of dysentery.

Why the barons turned to Louis

- ✓ John had some very powerful supporters, including the pope and William Marshal. By turning to France, the barons gained a powerful supporter.

- ✓ The king of France had more money to pay for the war – Louis would bring not only financial support but weapons and siege equipment which the rebels lacked.

- ✓ Louis would also bring experienced soldiers to bolster the rebel forces.

- ✓ Unlike loyal barons and John himself, few rebel barons had extensive military experience – Prince Louis did.

Now try this

Explain why Rochester Castle was important to a) King John, and b) the rebels.

John's death and the succession

John died in October 1216, before Prince Louis had totally defeated him in the civil war. He named his nine-year-old son Henry as his successor. England had been battered by civil war.

The problem of the succession

John had named 13 loyal barons who should rule as a council, but the succession of a child had often led to instability in the past. One member of the council, William Marshal, knew that Henry had to be crowned before the rebels crowned Louis. As London was in rebel hands, Henry was crowned in Gloucester on 28 October. The situation looked bleak for the royalists, though Henry had some advantages. Arguably the best of these was that on 11 November, the council elected William Marshal **Protector** and **regent**. Henry III had a powerful baron with great military experience and diplomatic skills to rule in his name.

The role of William Marshal as Protector

Marshal took Henry and the royal court to Bristol, where he issued an amended Magna Carta. This was a clever move, as Magna Carta now had the approval of the Church, and by agreeing to it, Marshal removed the rebel barons' original reasons for going to war. Some rebels switched sides, but by the end of 1216 the royalists still had serious disadvantages. The situation began to change in early 1217, when Louis returned to France for more troops and resources. This led more rebels to change sides, and the royalists began to win back control of the country. On 12 September 1217, peace was made and Louis gave up his claim to the throne.

Advantages of the rebels and Prince Louis	Advantages of the royalists
They directly controlled a large section of the country.	As he was so young, Henry had played no part in his father's reign, so the rebels could have no complaints against him.
Rebels held London – vital as the centre of trade.	Led by William Marshal as Protector and regent, the ruling council was made up of powerful barons with experience of warfare.
Land on the English side of the Scottish and Welsh borders was controlled by Llywelyn of Wales and Alexander II of Scotland.	Henry had the support of the Church. The papal legate (the pope's representative) arrived in November.
With French backing, they had more money than the royalists: England was almost bankrupt.	Most English people wanted an English king, not a French one, so Henry had popular support.
The rebels and the French greatly outnumbered the royalist forces.	John had built up the English navy, which was relatively strong.

Who ruled?
Parts were under control of the barons and Prince Louis of France. The borders of Wales and Scotland were under the control of Prince Llywelyn and Alexander II respectively. The rest of England was under royal control but was ruled by Protector William Marshal with the support of a council of nobles and the pope, as the king was just nine years old.

The condition of England by the end of 1216

How was the economy?
Trade, farming and all economic life had been seriously disrupted by civil war, so people were far worse off. The huge taxes and aids raised by John had left many short of money. The crown treasury had spent all the money it collected on war and was almost bankrupt.

Now try this

Give **four** reasons why Prince Louis of France didn't become king of England in 1216.

Exam overview

This page introduces you to the main features and requirements of the Paper 2 Option B2 exam.

About Paper 2

- Paper 2 is for both your period study and your British depth study.
- The reigns of King Richard I and King John is a British depth study – it will be in Section B of Paper 2: Medieval depth options.
- The reigns of King Richard I and King John is Option B2. You will see where it starts on the exam paper with a heading like this:

> Option B2: The reigns of King Richard I and King John, 1189–1216.

The Paper 2 exam lasts for 1 hour 45 minutes (105 minutes) in total. There are 32 marks for the period study and 32 marks for this depth study, so you should spend about 50 minutes on each.

The three questions

The three questions for Option B2 will always follow this pattern.

Question 5(a)

Describe **two** features of …　　　　**(4 marks)**

Question 5(a) targets Assessment Objective 1 (AO1): it focuses on describing features.

Assessment Objective 1 is where you show your knowledge and understanding of the key features and characteristics of The reigns of King Richard I and King John, 1189–1216.

You can see examples of all three questions on the next six pages, and in the practice questions on pages 38 to 49.

Question 5(b)

Explain why …　　　　**(12 marks)**

Two prompts and your own information

Question 5(b) targets both AO1 and Assessment Objective 2 (AO2). It focuses on causation: explaining why something happened.

Question 5(c)

Choice of two questions:
(c) (i) or (c) (ii)

[Statement] How far do you agree?
Explain your answer.　　　　**(16 marks)**

Two prompts and your own information

You have a choice of two questions for 5(c). These target both AO1 and AO2. You need to make a judgement in this question.

AO2 is where you explain and analyse key events using historical concepts such as causation, consequence, change, continuity, similarity and difference.

Question 5(a): Describing features 1

Question 5(a) on your exam paper will ask you to 'Describe **two** features of ...'. There are 4 marks available for this question: two for each feature you describe.

Worked example

Describe **two** features of the Interdict imposed on England in the years 1208–1213.   **(4 marks)**

 You can revise the Interdict on page 23.

What is a feature?

A **feature** is something that is distinctive or characteristic – we can tell one person from another, for example, because of their distinctive facial features. When a question asks for two features of something, think about the special characteristics of that something.

Sample answer

Feature 1

An Interdict was a punishment given to a country by the pope. The Interdict during John's reign was imposed by Pope Innocent III because of his dispute with King John over who should become the new archbishop of Canterbury.

Feature 2

It meant that people couldn't go to church for anything like marriages, burials or Sunday services.

There is no need to define what an Interdict is, as that is not required. Focus your answer on describing **features** of the Interdict.

Explaining why the Interdict was imposed by the pope is also not asked for in this question – you need to **describe** features.

Three features are actually identified here, but are only discussed briefly. You must focus on **two** features and give some detail about both.

Improved answer

Feature 1

The Interdict meant that people couldn't attend Sunday services in church. Many priests got around this by holding services in the churchyard or somewhere else outdoors.

Feature 2

The dead could not have a Christian burial in a church cemetery with a priest. Therefore people were buried in woods or other common ground without a priest present.

This correctly identifies one feature – 'couldn't attend Sunday services in church' – and includes supporting information.

This correctly identifies a second feature: 'could not receive Christian burials'. This answer focuses on two features and gives detail for both of them, which is all that's required.

Question 5(a): Describing features 2

Question 5(a) on your exam paper will ask you to 'Describe **two** features of ...'. There are 4 marks available for this question: two for each feature you describe.

Worked example

Describe **two** features of a peasant's life between 1189 and 1216.   **(4 marks)**

🔗 **Links** You can revise rural life on page 10.

What does 'describe' mean?

Describe means give an account of the main characteristics of something. You develop your description with relevant details, but you do not need to include reasons or justifications.

Sample answer

Feature 1

Peasants worked the land.

This has identified a feature, but is very vague. Supporting information needs to be added.

Feature 2

Religion and going to church were important to all people at this time. People had Sundays off to go to church, and other holidays were around the time of festivals, such as Christmas.

This describes a feature of life at the time, but needs to be made more specific to peasants, as the question asks.

Improved answer

Feature 1

All peasants, whether free or unfree, men, women and children, worked the land all year around to provide food for themselves and for everyone else.

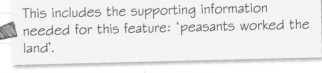

This includes the supporting information needed for this feature: 'peasants worked the land'.

Feature 2

Sunday was their only day off to go to church, and other holidays were around the time of festivals, such as Christmas.

This correctly describes how religion was a feature of peasants' lives at this time. Make sure you focus your answers on the exact question asked.

Question 5(b): Explaining why 1

Question 5(b) on your exam paper is about causation: explaining why something happened. There are 12 marks available for this question, and two prompts to help you answer. You must also use information of your own.

Worked example

Explain why King John took so long to reconcile with the pope. **(12 marks)**

You may use the following in your answer:
- the plot of 1212
- confiscation of Church property.

You **must** also use information of your own.

Links You can revise the dispute with the papacy on pages 22–24.

What does 'explain' mean?

Explain means saying how or why something happened, backed up with examples or justifications to support the reasons you give. Good ways to get into an explanation are to use sentence starters like, 'One reason for this was …' or 'This was because …'

Compare this answer extract with an improved version on the next page.

Sample extract

The dispute between King John and Pope Innocent III began in 1205 when they disagreed over who should become the next archbishop of Canterbury. They were not reconciled until 1213, when John agreed to the pope's terms for reconciliation and even went further by becoming the pope's vassal for his land in England and Ireland. The main reasons why it took so long was because John did not want to back down, and also he was gaining financially from the dispute. He only reconciled when he saw it was in his interest to do so.

Pope Innocent III was determined to assert his authority over John, but John was equally adamant that he should be able to appoint his own archbishops as other kings had before him. Neither wanted to back down.

King John gained a lot financially from the dispute, so he was in no hurry to reconcile with him. He confiscated the property of any clergy who sided with the pope rather than him. This meant that he gained the profits from that land. He also gained money from fines the clergy had to pay to get their land back or to be released after John had had them arrested.

The situation changed in 1212 when John became aware that some of his leading barons, Robert Fitz Walter and Eustace de Vesci, and Prince Llywelyn of Wales, were plotting to kill him. The barons had become increasingly angry with John throughout his reign, but John did little to improve relations until after this plot, when he eased some of the tax demanded of them. It was also at this point that he decided a reconciliation would be beneficial, as he needed allies and the pope was a powerful ally.

Set out your line of argument early on. The first half of this paragraph includes a bit too much detail for this stage of the answer.

Using your own knowledge is **essential**. This student shows thorough knowledge of both the pope and King John, and the dispute between them (AO1). You also need to **link** that knowledge explicitly to an explanation (AO2), which is only hinted at here: 'neither wanted to back down'.

Use the prompts in the question to help you; here, the student has used the second prompt: confiscation of Church property. The answer again shows good knowledge (AO1), but still only a brief attempt ('so he was in no hurry to reconcile with him') at explanation.

This paragraph shows better explanation (AO2). You need to show both knowledge (AO1) and explanation (AO2) **throughout** your answer.

Question 5(b): Explaining why 2

This page has an improved version of the answer given on the previous page.

Improved extract

The dispute between King John and Pope Innocent III began in 1205; they were not reconciled until 1213, when John sought reconciliation. The main reasons why it took so long for John to do this was because he did not want to back down and also he was gaining financially from the dispute. He only reconciled with the pope when he realised it was in his self-interest to do so.

Pope Innocent III was determined to assert his authority over John, but John was equally determined that he should be able to appoint his own archbishops as other kings had before him. This was a major reason why reconciliation took so long: neither wanted to back down. Also, John had the support of most of the population of England in his dispute with Innocent – it would have been much harder to continue the dispute without this support.

King John's main focus during these years was gathering as much money as possible in order to try to regain his lands in France. The dispute with the pope actually gave John an opportunity to make more money. He confiscated the property of any clergy who sided with the pope rather than him, so he gained the profits from that land. He also gained money from fines the clergy had to pay to get their land back or to be released after John had had them arrested. Therefore, John gained a lot financially from the dispute with the pope, so he was in no hurry to reconcile with him as he wanted to continue making as much money as possible.

Before 1212, King John did not have a lot to gain from reconciling with the pope, but this changed when John became aware that some of his leading barons, Robert Fitz Walter and Eustace de Vesci, and Prince Llywelyn of Wales, were plotting to kill him. The barons had become increasingly angry with John, but the king did little to improve relations with his barons until after this plot, when he eased some of the tax demanded of them. It was also at this point that he decided reconciling with the pope would be beneficial as he needed allies and the pope was the most powerful ally.

Causation questions

Question 5(b) is about causation – causes. These questions have 6 marks for AO1 (accurate and relevant information) and 6 marks for AO2 (explanation and analysis). Strong answers combine explanation and analysis (AO2) with relevant information (AO1).

The first paragraph should focus on the line of argument you are going to take, as this does. The student has taken out the unnecessary detail.

The second paragraph adds more than the previous answer to clearly explain why reconciliation took so long. It adds another reason: the support of most of the population.

This third paragraph now includes more explanation (AO2) as well as good use of own knowledge (AO1). The student explains why gaining money was so important for John at this time and therefore why he was in 'no hurry' to reconcile with the pope before he did.

Again, this paragraph now includes more explanation. The answer should go on to mention the threat of French invasion in 1213, which was another trigger for John reconciling with the pope as he needed the pope on his side rather than with France.

Analysis is about examining something carefully in order to identify the reasons that explain it. The most successful answers to 5(b) questions provide an analytical explanation. This means a tight focus on what the question is asking, and careful selection of reasons that provide a well-considered explanation.

Question 5(c): Making a judgement 1

Question 5(c) on your exam paper involves analysing the statement in the question and deciding how far you agree with it. There are 16 marks available for this question and two prompts to help you answer. You must also use information of your own.

Worked example

'The main reason Richard was able to regain most of his land in France by his death was his military skill.'

How far do you agree? Explain your answer.   **(16 marks)**

You may use the following in your answer:
- Chateau Gaillard
- Counts of Toulouse, Flanders and Boulogne.

You **must** also use information of your own.

 Links You can revise Richard's regaining of Normandy on pages 19–20.

Analysing the statement

Question 5(c) will always include a statement, which may start with phrases such as 'The main reason for ...' or 'The main consequence of ...' You decide whether you agree or not by considering whether other aspects or reasons, or other consequences, were more important.

Compare this answer with an improved version on the next page.

Sample answer

Richard's military skill was an important factor in him being able to regain most of his land in France by the time of his death. Philip II of France had taken control of many important castles and most of western Normandy. Richard's skill in siege warfare won back many castles from Philip. Richard's skill as a warrior helped to inspire his troops. This was important in, for example, preventing Philip's forces from taking the castle of Verneuil. Richard's bravery was also evident at Vendome, where he inflicted a humiliating defeat on Philip, nearly catching Philip himself, in July 1194.

Richard's skill as a military strategist led him to build Chateau Gaillard between 1196–98. The castle was in a strategically important position, so Richard could defend Normandy from it. It was regarded as having the best defences in western Europe. It was also in a great place for launching attacks on Philip's lands, and enabled Richard to retake almost all the Vexin (a strategically important area in northern France) by the time of his death.

Richard's military skill was not the only reason why he was able to regain most of his land in France, however. For example, Richard made alliances with other foreign leaders and managed to persuade many barons who were supporting Philip to change sides and support him again. However, I agree that Richard's military skill was the most important reason why he was able to pass on to his successor most of the land that he had lost.

Discussing the reason mentioned in the statement is a good way to start your answer. This student gives a good overview, as well as providing specific examples. If anything, it is too detailed.

The student uses one of the bullet points in the question: Chateau Gaillard. This is fine: you do not have to use the bullet points but you must include your own information.

This shows good knowledge of Chateau Gaillard (AO1) and links this to Richard's military skill, which is what the question requires.

 This answer provides good knowledge (AO1) of the reason given in the question, but there is not enough analysis of other reasons – you need to consider other reasons before deciding how far you agree with the statement.

 Make sure you come to a conclusion. State clearly how far you agree with the statement in the question.

Question 5(c): Making a judgement 2

This page has an improved version of the answer to 5(c)(i) on the previous page.

Improved answer

Richard's military skill was an important factor in him being able to regain most of his land in France by the time of his death. Richard's skill in siege warfare won back many castles from Philip, and his skill and bravery as a warrior helped to inspire his troops to win battles in the open, too.

However, military skill was not the only reason Richard was able to regain control of much of his land in France. Many nobles had switched allegiance to Philip and were supporting him when Richard returned to France in 1194. Richard used bribery and negotiation to win back the support of many nobles. This meant that Richard had more knights under his control who could fight for him and not Philip. He also forged alliances with foreign rulers, such as the counts of Toulouse, Flanders and Boulogne, which cut off financial and military support for Philip from elsewhere, as well as bringing this support to his own side. These two factors would not have driven back the French forces without Richard's military skill, however.

Strategy was an important part of Richard's military skill. This led him to build Chateau Gaillard (1196–98) in a strategically important position for defending Normandy from French attack. It was also in a great place for launching attacks on Philip's lands, and enabled Richard to retake almost all the Vexin (a strategically important area in northern France) by the time of his death.

In conclusion, Richard's military skill was not the only reason why he was able to regain most of his land in France, but I agree that it was the main reason. Making alliances with other foreign leaders and bribing many barons who were supporting Philip to change sides and support him both contributed, but needed Richard's military skill to actually win back the land lost and drive the French back.

The balance of Assessment Objectives

Question 5(c) is worth 16 marks in total. Of this, 6 marks are for AO1 and 10 marks for AO2, which shows the importance of analysis and explanation. AO1 information and understanding also needs to be combined with AO2 for the best results.

Discussion of the reason mentioned in the statement is now condensed in this opening paragraph, allowing other factors to be discussed.

The answer now moves on to analyse two other factors the student considers to be important: forging foreign alliances and bribing nobles to change sides. It then evaluates the importance of military skill against these other factors.

Remember, for question 5(c) in the exam you will choose to answer **either** option (i) **or** option (ii). Each option targets both AO1 and AO2.

The solid analysis leads to a concluding paragraph with a judgement.

Practice

Put your skills and knowledge into practice with the following question.

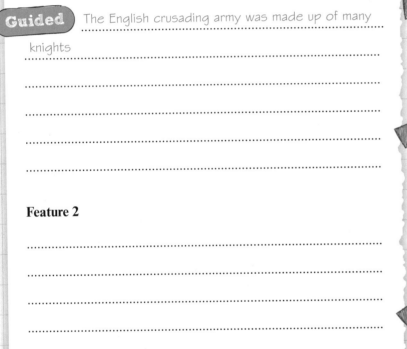

Option B2: The reigns of King Richard I and King John, 1189–1216

Answer Questions 5(a), 5(b) and **EITHER** 5(c)(i) **OR** 5(c)(ii).

5 **(a)** Describe **two** features of the English crusading army that went on the Third Crusade.　　　**(4 marks)**

Feature 1

Guided　The English crusading army was made up of many

knights

....

....

....

....

Feature 2

....

....

....

....

....

....

You have 1 hour 45 minutes for the **whole** of Paper 2, so you should spend about **50 minutes** on this option. Remember to leave 5 minutes or so to check your work when you've finished writing.

Links You can revise the English crusading army on page 14.

This question is only worth 4 marks, so don't spend too long on your answer: you just need to identify **two** valid features and support each one.

An example of a suitable feature might be 'the English crusading army was made up of many knights who were fulfilling knight service ...'. A suitable support statement could be '... to their lord, who owed the king knights in return for their fief.'

Your exam paper will have a separate space for each feature you need to describe.

Describe means you have to give an account of the main characteristic. You do not need to explain why the feature was important or what it was trying to achieve.

Practice

Put your skills and knowledge into practice with the following question.

5 (b) Explain why it took King John time to secure power after Richard I's death in 1199. **(12 marks)**

You may use the following in your answer:

- Prince Arthur, Duke of Brittany
- Philip II's invasion of Normandy.

You **must** also use information of your own.

....

....

....

....

....

....

....

....

....

....

....

....

....

....

....

....

....

....

....

....

....

....

....

Remember that question 5(b) is all about causation: this means you are looking for relevant reasons.

Links You can revise how John secured power on page 8.

For example, you might explain that the throne was also claimed by Prince Arthur, Duke of Brittany, who was the son of John's elder brother who had died. Although most English barons supported John's claim, many barons in the areas of France that had been ruled by Richard I supported Arthur's claim.

There are 12 marks on offer for this question. You don't have to use the prompts in the question in your answer but you **must** include your own information to answer the question fully.

Your explanations need to stay focused on answering the question. Although you might remember a lot of detail about John securing power, you need to focus on providing **reasons why** it took some time, not descriptions of what happened.

Practice

Use this page to continue your answer to question 5(b).

For example, you might explain that Philip II invaded Normandy soon after Richard I's death **because** he wanted to claim Normandy for France. In order for John to secure his throne, he had to go to war with Philip and drive the French forces out of Normandy, which he did, making peace at Le Goulet in 1200.

Remember: the best answers to Question 5(b) will show a good knowledge of the key features and characteristics of the period **and** analyse causation. They will also show how factors combine with each other to bring about an outcome – so in this case how different factors came together to make it difficult for John to secure the throne.

Make sure you support your explanation with a good range of accurate and relevant detail throughout your answer.

Practice

Put your skills and knowledge into practice with the following question.

Answer EITHER 5(c)(i) OR 5(c)(ii).

EITHER

5 (c) (i) 'The main reason people joined the Third Crusade was to gain financially.'

How far do you agree?

Explain your answer. **(16 marks)**

You may use the following in your answer:

- indulgence
- knight service.

You **must** also use information of your own.

OR

5 (c) (ii) 'King John's death in October 1216 was the main reason why Prince Louis of France never became king of England.'

How far do you agree?

Explain your answer. **(16 marks)**

You may use the following in your answer:

- William Marshal
- Pope Innocent III

You **must** also use information of your own.

For **Question 5(c)**, you have a **choice of two questions**. Each question is worth the same number of marks. Although one might immediately seem a question you can answer, do read both carefully to check that your choice is the right one.

On the exam paper, the two options for Question 5(c) will be on one page, and you will then turn to the next page to write your answer – like the layout here.

If you decide to answer 5(c)(i), turn to page 42. If you decide to answer 5(c)(ii), turn to page 46.

Links You can revise reasons for going on crusade on page 14. For more about the succession after John's death, turn to page 30.

Choosing a question

At the top of the first answer page there will be an instruction for you to indicate which of the two questions you have chosen to answer. You do this by making a cross in the box for 5(c)(i) or 5(c)(ii). (You can see this on page 42 and 46.) Don't worry if you put a cross in the wrong box by mistake. Just put a line through the cross and then put a new cross in the correct box.

Practice

Put your skills and knowledge into practice with the following question.

Indicate which question you are answering by marking a cross in the box. If you change your mind, put a line through the box and then indicate your new question with a cross.

Chosen question: 5(c)(i) ☒   5(c)(ii) ☐

Guided

There were many reasons why people joined the Third Crusade. They included financial gain, as many hoped to benefit from the crusade by gaining wealth but also by not paying various debts or taxes while they were on crusade.

....
....
....
....
....
....
....
....
....
....
....
....
....
....
....
....
....
....
....
....
....
....

Plan your answer **before** you start writing. List factors that support the statement in the question, and list other factors that go against the statement.

For example:

Support	Against
Opportunities to gain wealth and land in the Holy Land	Many went to complete knight service
Wouldn't have to pay the Saladin tithe	Religious reasons including indulgence
Crusaders' debts were postponed until they returned	To win glory and go on an adventure

Spending a couple of minutes planning your answer means you can write an introduction setting up your arguments.

For each point you make, always go on to explain how it relates to the question.

Practice

Use this page to continue your answer to question 5(c)(i).

....
....
....
....
....
....
....
....
....
....
....
....
....
....
....
....
....
....
....
....
....
....
....
....
....
....
....
....
....
....
....
....
....

Remember **only** to answer **either** Question 5(c)(i) **or** Question 5(c)(ii) in the exam.

As with question 5(b), you do not have to use both or either of the two prompts provided in the question. If you do use them, remember that you **must** also include information of your own.

End your answer by saying **how far** you agree with the question statement, and give support for your decision.

For example, you might conclude that financial gain was just one reason why people joined the Third Crusade, rather than being their main reason for joining.

Practice

Use this page to continue your answer to question 5(c)(i).

....

....

....

....

....

....

....

....

....

....

....

....

....

....

....

....

....

....

....

....

....

....

....

....

....

....

....

....

Practice

Use this page to continue your answer to question 5(c)(i).

....
....
....
....
....
....
....
....
....
....
....
....
....
....
....
....
....
....
....
....
....
....
....
....
....
....
....
....
....

Practice

Put your skills and knowledge into practice with the following question.

Indicate which question you are answering by marking a cross in the box. If you change your mind, put a line through the box and then indicate your new question with a cross.

Chosen question: 5(c)(i) ☐   5(c)(ii) ☒

Guided   King John's death was at least partly responsible

for Prince Louis of France not becoming king. John died

before Louis had totally defeated him, so John's heir, Henry,

was able to become king. If John had lived, Louis might

have totally defeated him and taken over the rest of the

country, in which case he would very likely have become

king. However, there were other reasons why Louis did not

become king

....

....

....

....

....

....

....

....

....

....

....

....

....

....

....

....

Remember, Question 5(c) gives you a choice of two questions. **In the exam, you only need to answer either 5(c)(i) or 5(c)(ii).**

This question asks about **reasons**. This means you need to think of the reasons why Prince Louis of France never became king of England, and then analyse how important each reason was. There may also be links between the reasons.

For example, if John had lived, William Marshal would not have become Protector and England might not have benefited from the good decisions he made, such as reissuing Magna Carta.

Practice

Use this page to continue your answer to question 5(c)(ii).

As with question 5(b), you do not have to use both or either of the two prompts provided by the question. If you do use them, remember that you **must** also include information of your own.

Bring specific facts and details into your answer to show how well you understand the key features and characteristics that are involved in the question.

When you end your answer, make sure you say **how far** you agree with the question statement, and give support for your decision.

Practice

Use this page to continue your answer to question 5(c)(ii).

Practice

Use this page to continue your answer to question 5(c)(ii).

....

....

....

....

....

....

....

....

....

....

....

....

....

....

....

....

....

....

....

....

....

....

....

.... Practice

....

....

Answers

Where an example answer is given, this is not necessarily the only correct response. In most cases there is a range of responses that can gain full marks.

SUBJECT CONTENT

Life and government in England, 1189–1216

The feudal system

1. The feudal hierarchy

Any two descriptions from the following are valid:

- A vassal held land granted him by his lord.
- A vassal paid homage to their lord.
- A vassal provided services to their lord.
- A vassal came under their lord's protection.

2. The nature of feudalism

Forfeiture (loss of land) occurred when vassals did not provide the services required of them to their lord, or when a vassal broke their oath of loyalty to the lord. It was designed to protect the interest of the lord – if the vassal did something the lord didn't like, the lord could take away the source of the vassal's power and wealth. This kept the king firmly in charge of his tenants-in-chief, and the tenants-in-chief firmly in charge of the under-tenants.

3. Role and influence of the Church

The Church held huge amounts of land from the king. This land earned the Church money through rent paid by free peasants, nobles or knights who leased land, as well as profits made on the produce of the land. Everyone paid a tithe in produce (a tenth of what they made) to the Church as well. Another source of revenue was donations of money or land that people gave as offerings or in their wills.

The Church's wealth gave it power and influence over the king because it was a large taxpayer to the king. The king needed this tax, so he was careful to avoid doing things the Church disagreed with and to take advice from leading churchmen. Its wealth also gave the Church power and influence over people generally, because many people depended on the Church for their own food, housing, land, employment, etc.

Kingship and succession

4. The nature of kingship

Rituals gave people the chance to see the king and for him to display his power and authority. Some rituals took place in cathedrals, to emphasise the idea that the king had been chosen by God and that his subjects should therefore show him loyalty and obedience.

5. Richard I as king

Richard was the obvious choice:

- he had experience of ruling a large area as Duke of Aquitaine

- he was the eldest surviving son of the king who had just died – Henry II
- he was already a successful military leader, which was seen as an essential quality for a king
- he was really the only option.

6. John as king

Richard was clearly the leading candidate for the throne. John's claim was not as clear-cut, as some leading barons supported his nephew Arthur rather than John. However, they were mainly in Angevin lands in France rather than in England. Also, Arthur had the powerful support of Philip II of France, and Philip invaded the important region of Normandy as soon as he heard Richard had died, as he wanted to claim it for himself – challenging John as king very early on.

Royal government and finances

7. England under Richard

Evidence that Richard ruled England well includes the following:

- he set up stable government before leaving on crusade
- he appointed able men to rule in his absence
- although he was rarely in England, he still oversaw government by corresponding with those he'd left in charge, particularly when in France after 1194.

Evidence that Richard ruled England badly includes the following:

- he was hardly in the country; some argue he took little interest in it except as a source of revenue for his crusade and wars in France
- he appointed William Longchamp to rule in his absence, which later proved to be a poor choice
- he failed to control John's actions.

8. England under John

Any three reasons from the following are valid:

- The barons' traditional role of advising the king was done by 'new men' instead of English barons, which the English barons resented.
- The increase in tax and money they had to pay John.
- They blamed John for losing Normandy.
- They feared his cruel punishments of barons who had displeased him (for example, de Braose).
- As John took almost complete control over the justice system, they saw him as applying the law to benefit himself and not applying it fairly to them.
- John's dispute with the pope may have angered some.

9. Royal revenues

Similarities include:

- Both used traditional ways of raising royal revenues through increasing taxes.

- Both used the feudal incidents at their disposal, for example tenants-in-chief paid money towards Richard's ransom.
- Both collected forest fines, inheritance fines and wardship fines.
- Both used scutage to hire professional soldiers for wars in France; both sold offices; both created aids to pay for 'exceptional circumstances', for example for Richard's ransom and John's tax on moveables and income to raise money for war in France in 1207.

Differences include:

- John created some totally new ways of raising finance, such as his tax on moveables and income.
- Richard charged men to retain the offices they had bought previously.
- John hugely increased money due from feudal incidents, especially forest fines and wardship fines.
- John raised scutage more often than Richard, and raised the amount due per knight to be paid.
- John 'sold justice'.
- John's ways of raising money fell heavily on the barons and put many of them in debt.

English society

10. Rural medieval England

A description of any two features from the following is valid:

- All peasants (men, women and children) worked on the land – for their lord and for themselves.
- They received land from their lord on which to grow food for their own families, either in return for labour service (for unfree peasants) or for rent (for freemen).
- They worked hard to grow food for themselves and their lord. At times of poor harvest they were vulnerable to food shortages and even famine.
- They kept animals to provide food and clothing for themselves and sometimes to sell. Animals were kept on common land during the day and in the peasants' houses at night to protect them from predators.
- The peasants worked on the land all year round, every day except for Sundays and religious holidays.

11. Medieval towns

A description of any two features from the following is valid:

- Towns were where people could sell surplus food they had grown or goods they had made. They were where people made money to buy things they could not make or grow themselves.
- Towns were where most craftspeople lived and worked, providing important goods for people as well as generating revenue for the country.
- Towns were the centre of all national and international trade. Food, raw materials and goods, such as textiles, were bought and sold. Trade was essential to the national economy.

- Towns generated a great deal of revenue for the king through tallage, customs duties, tolls on sales and purchases, and tolls to use gateways and roads.

12. Jews in medieval England

Any three causes from the following are valid:

- Long-standing hatred of Jews as non-Christians and because, according to the Bible, they were the people who had killed Jesus. Also, more recent rumours across Europe of Jewish rituals involving the killing of Christian children.
- Jealousy and resentment at Jewish success in business.
- Many resented owing Jews money.
- People were afraid of difference – Jews dressing differently, having different festivals, religious rites, etc.
- The Crusades heightened differences between Christians and other faiths. Richard I left on crusade in December 1189. There was a lot of anti-Jewish as well as anti-Muslim propaganda to try to persuade people to accompany Richard on crusade.
- The short-term trigger was the anger of some Christians who were offended because some Jews tried to give Richard I a coronation present.

Involvements overseas, 1189–1204

The nature of crusading

13. Causes of the Third Crusade

Crusader states – the regions in the Holy Land captured during the First Crusade and then ruled by Christians. The Third Crusade was launched to defend the crusader states from Muslim attack, especially the Kingdom of Jerusalem, which had been retaken by Muslim forces.

Papal bull – an official announcement/declaration made by the pope. The papal bull of October 1187 called for a Third Crusade to take back Jerusalem from Muslims.

Indulgence – indulgences were given by the Church to people who had done good deeds, they reduced the time people would spend in purgatory being punished for their sins. A full indulgence was basically a passage straight to heaven after death and forgiveness of all sin. The pope promised a full indulgence to anyone who went on the Third Crusade

Jerusalem – a holy city for Christians, Muslims and Jews. It was located in the Kingdom of Jerusalem, one of the crusader states. The Kingdom of Jerusalem, including the city of Jerusalem, had been retaken by Muslim forces and the Third Crusade was launched to get it back under Christian control.

14. The English crusading army

Although knights had to pay the costs of going on crusade, it could be financially beneficial because of the wealth that could be gained in the Holy Land. Victorious crusaders could take the possessions and valuables of those they defeated. There was also the possibility of obtaining land in newly conquered areas. Going on crusade also offered a way out of repaying debts (which were postponed until crusaders returned) and a way to avoid paying the Saladin tithe.

Richard, the Crusader King

15. Richard and the Third Crusade

Any three reasons from the following are valid:

- Richard refused to give Philip an equal share of the spoils in Sicily, and refused to give him anything from Cyprus.
- Richard married Berengaria of Navarre instead of Philip's sister as had been agreed.
- They disagreed over who should be the next king of Jerusalem.
- Richard paid his professional soldiers more than Philip.
- Both wanted to lead the crusade, especially after Frederick I drowned.

16. Victories at Acre and Arsuf

Any two examples from the following are valid:

- Richard showed great courage and personal bravery, especially during the Battle of Arsuf (which would have inspired his men).
- He showed great leadership in keeping the crusaders together during the tough conditions on the march to Jaffa.
- He showed great tactical skill, especially during the march to Jaffa and the Battle of Arsuf.

17. Failure to recapture Jerusalem

The main reasons were that Jerusalem was well defended with a wall and fortresses around the city; leaving the coast meant that Saladin's army could have surrounded the crusaders and cut off their supply lines; laying siege successfully would have been very difficult and would probably have required more troops than the crusaders had at this time, and it would have required even more troops to defend the city once they had won it.

In addition, weather conditions hampered both the marches on Jerusalem: during the first march, heavy rain made progress slow and destroyed food, clothes and weapons; during the second march, hot weather increased fears of a lack of water.

Aftermath of the crusade

18. Richard's return and capture

An explanation of any three ways from the following is valid:

- Jews had to pay a tallage of £3375.
- A one-off land tax on all tenants-in-chief and under-tenants was charged.
- A one-off tax of 25 per cent on income and moveables (goods) was charged.
- The king of Scotland gave £1350.
- Gold and silver were taken from all churches in England.
- Cistercian monks had to give the crown a year's supply of wool.

Richard, John and Normandy

19. Competing aims in Normandy

Any three reasons from the following are valid:

- Normandy was an important gateway to other regions in France.
- Normandy was close to the French capital, Paris, so it was strategically important.
- Normandy was close to England – an important link for Richard and John to their other French lands, and a launching point for a potential invasion of England for Philip.
- It had very fertile farmland providing crops and animal fodder.
- Norman towns were centres of trade, providing revenue to whichever king owned them.

20. Chateau Gaillard

The main reason was to defend Rouen, and therefore Normandy as a whole, from French attack. Other reasons would have been to provide a good base from which to attack French castles in the Vexin and also to provide a magnificent royal palace to hold court.

21. John's loss of Normandy

John can be blamed for:

- leaving Normandy rather than staying to lead the defence in December 1203
- poor military strategy, such as when he failed to send relief to Chateau Gaillard
- swearing fealty to Philip in 1200: accepting he was Philip's vassal meant that Philip could then treat him as such, and tenants-in-chief in France could then treat Philip as their overlord
- failure to compensate Hugh de Lusignan for the loss of Isabelle of Angouleme, who had been promised to him in marriage, which sparked the war in the first place
- mistreating prisoners, especially his nephew, Arthur, which angered many nobles and made them switch sides.

He cannot be blamed for:

- Philip's military and diplomatic skills
- lack of money (due to Richard's wars), which meant he couldn't afford more professional soldiers or pay bribes to maintain alliances
- the English barons being unwilling to help him due to lack of money and an unwillingness to fight more wars.

King John's downfall, 1205–16

The dispute with the papacy

22. John vs the papacy: causes

John disagreed with the way Langton had been chosen, as he had had no input in the choice – the pope had chosen Langton. John firmly believed that he should be able to choose his bishops as his brother, father and other medieval kings had done.

John also disagreed with Langton at a personal level because he had been living in Paris for a long time and had enjoyed the patronage of Philip II, who John saw as his great enemy and had seized Normandy from him.

John wanted John de Gray, Bishop of Norwich, to become archbishop. Like other kings before him, he told the monks of Canterbury who he wanted, and expected them to agree with his choice.

23. The Interdict

Interdict is a suspension of all Church services and most of the Christian sacraments for people living in the country/area where it is imposed. **Excommunication** applies to an individual; it denies that person all Christian sacraments and means they will go to hell when they die.

24. John vs the papacy: reconciliation

For the pope, the benefits were that it appeared as though he had 'won' and achieved everything he wanted and more: John had agreed to become his vassal and held his kingdoms as fiefs.

For John, the benefits were that it gave him a very powerful ally, which would discourage a French invasion, and put him under the protection of the pope, which would be useful in future conflicts or quarrels with others.

Worsening relations with the barons

25. Financial burdens

Any three of the following are valid:

- Demanding scutage an unprecedented number of times put the barons under a lot of financial pressure.
- Increasing, often dramatically, the amount due on fines for things such as wardship and inheritance.
- New taxes, such as the thirteenth, which was collected in 1207, often fell heavily on the barons.
- Widows were treated harshly and had to pay large fines or marry someone chosen by the king.
- John's use of the justice system to benefit himself – use of arbitrary power
- Cruel and degrading punishments on barons and their families, for example, William de Braose.
- Selling justice so that those who paid John won their law cases.
- The disagreement with the papacy – especially the excommunication, which forced the barons to choose between the pope and the king.
- Using 'new men' instead of barons to advise him.
- Allegations that John tried to seduce the barons' wives and daughters.
- Failing to regain Normandy.

26. The 1212 plot and failure in Normandy

Barons were angry because military defeat seemed to prove John's nickname of 'softsword' – medieval kings were supposed to be good warriors. Also, many of the barons would have hoped to regain or gain land for themselves in Normandy if it had been won back. Defeat ensured that France would become more powerful, which many barons would have disliked. Probably the most anger was caused by the huge financial burden imposed by the campaign in Normandy. John had raised the largest ever scutage, plus taxes and fines, to pay for it, and it had come to nothing.

Magna Carta and the First Barons' War

27. The rebellion of 1215

It could be argued that the key moment was the rebellion turning to warfare in Northampton. Most historians believe that the rebels taking London was the major event that made John agree first to talk with the barons and then to sign Magna Carta. As well as being the seat of government, it was also the centre of England's wealth and therefore of John's revenue. He and the rebel barons realised that without London, John would find winning a war much more difficult, even though he was still in the ascendancy.

28. Runnymede

Reasons **for the statement** include:

- most of the provisions directly address the barons' grievances
- several provisions would give the barons far more power, for example, the creation of a council of barons; tax could only be levied with their agreement
- the only reason other people/bodies, such as the Church and freemen, were included was so that the rebel barons would gain more supporters.

Reasons **against the statement** include:

- the provisions on the freedom of the Church did not benefit the barons
- several provisions were explicitly worded for 'everyone', so would not just have benefited the barons (for example, justice couldn't be sold or denied to anyone)
- several provisions are directed at all freemen, so would have benefited knights and merchants as well as barons.

29. The outbreak of war

Rochester Castle was important to both sides because it was on the road from Dover to London.

a) If John could capture it, he could prevent Louis' forces from reaching London. It would also be a good place to launch an attack to try to retake London.

b) It provided the best place for defending the road to London and therefore London itself. Holding London was essential if the barons were to have any chance of success.

The succession

30. John's death and the succession

Any four reasons from the following are valid:

- King John's death meant that Louis never totally defeated him in battle. Although the rebel army controlled a large section of the country, including London, the crown still controlled a substantial part.

- John's successor, his son Henry, was too young to have been associated with his father's unpopular policies. The rebel barons had no complaints against him.
- Louis was French, and most English people wanted an English king. France was still seen as the 'enemy'.
- The excellent leadership of William Marshal for the royalists.
- Louis didn't have the support of the pope. The pope supported Henry, and a papal legate supported William Marshal and the rest of the council's decisions.
- Henry was crowned quickly, before the rebels could crown Louis.
- The reissuing of Magna Carta meant that the barons' issues with the king had been resolved. Many switched sides and deserted Louis once Magna Carta had been approved.

PRACTICE

38. Practice

5(a) For each feature, you get one mark for identifying the feature up to a maximum of two features and one mark for adding supporting information, for example:

The English crusading army was made up of many knights (1 mark) who were fulfilling their knight service to their lord in return for their land (1 mark).

Your two features could include points and supporting information from the following – yellow highlight indicates features and green highlight indicates supporting information:

- The largest number of people were members of a knight's household, such as knights' squires who worked for the knights on crusade by, for example, looking after their horses.
- The army included many priests, some of whom fought. All provided spiritual support for the rest of the army.
- Some professional soldiers went on crusade. They were hired mercenaries, experienced in warfare, who were paid to go.
- Civilians, including some knights' wives, went on crusade. They played no role in the actual fighting but helped the army in other ways, such as cooking and providing medical help.
- Some important people went on crusade, including some barons and important churchmen.

39. Practice

5(b) There are 6 marks on offer for AO1 and 6 marks for AO2 in this question. If you do not introduce your own information, you can only get a maximum of 8 marks. Your AO1 information needs to be accurate and relevant and your AO2 needs to provide an explanation of the question.

Points that you make in your explanation could include:

- There was a rival claim to the throne whose claim was stronger according to primogeniture: Prince Arthur of Brittany, the son of John's elder brother (Geoffrey) who had died. Arthur claimed he was the rightful king.

- John's powerful mother (Arthur's grandmother), Eleanor of Aquitaine, supported John's claim and most barons in Aquitaine supported John, but many in other parts of France supported Arthur. Arthur's most powerful supporter was Philip II, king of France. Philip supported Arthur's claim to the throne because Arthur had grown up in the French court, and Phillip believed he could influence Arthur, as he was young.
- Philip II invaded Normandy soon after hearing of Richard's death. Arthur did homage to Philip for lands in France, except for Normandy which Philip wanted for himself. John quickly went to France with an army and started trying to drive the French back out of Normandy. In May 1200, peace was made with Philip at Le Goulet, and Philip and Arthur finally acknowledged John as king.
- There was also potential for invasion of England by Scotland, as the Scottish king wanted land in England. John charged a loyal and powerful baron (who had plenty of knights under his service) to protect it so there was no invasion.

42. Practice

5(c)(i) questions have 16 marks on offer: 6 for AO1 and 10 for AO2. Your task is to evaluate the statement and reach a conclusion as to the extent to which you agree with it, justifying your conclusion. This means considering how important the reason given in the statement is compared to other reasons.

You might support the statement with points like the following:

- Knights often profited financially from going to war, both by taking the possessions of the losing side and civilians (the 'spoils of war'), and also by gaining land given to them after victory. There was a lot of land available in the Holy Land. This may have been a particular incentive for younger brothers of noble families, who did not have land of their own.
- Mercenaries were professional soldiers who were highly experienced fighters. Richard paid for many mercenaries to accompany him on crusade, and these men were undoubtedly motivated by money as they made a living from fighting.
- The other financial incentive for going on crusade was that it was a way of avoiding payments that were due. Crusaders did not have to pay the crusading tax (known as the Saladin tithe), and their debts were postponed until they returned from crusade.

You might disagree with the statement with points like the following:

- Most people were religious at the time, so religious reasons would have been a major motivation for many crusaders, not just the clergy who went on crusade themselves. Many Christians felt it was their religious duty to try to regain Christian control of Jerusalem, the holiest place in Christianity. The pope promised all crusaders a full indulgence, meaning they would go straight to heaven when they died rather than spending time in purgatory. This would have been a strong motivating factor. Members of the clergy spent a lot of time persuading people to go on crusade.

- Some people may have been motivated by revenge, as they believed Muslims were infidels, and Jerusalem needed 'saving'. Tales of Muslim atrocities, which were usually untrue, were told to persuade people to go.

- Many knights probably saw the crusade as an opportunity to win glory and respect at a time when being a good warrior was highly valued.

- It was also a great opportunity for adventure and a chance to see other places and cultures at a time when not many people had the opportunity to do this. Most Christians would have wanted to see Jerusalem and other sacred places in the Holy Land.

- Most crusaders probably chose to go on crusade for a variety of reasons, so although financial incentives may have played a part, they are unlikely to have been a major factor for most crusaders.

46. Practice

5(c)(ii) questions have 16 marks on offer: 6 for AO1 and 10 for AO2. Your task is to evaluate the statement and reach a conclusion as to the extent to which you agree with it, justifying your conclusion. This means considering how important the reason given in the statement is compared to other reasons.

You might support the statement with points like the following:

- King John's death came at a time when Prince Louis and the rebel barons were making great gains across England. In all likelihood this would have continued if John had lived and continued to rule. In that event, John would probably have been defeated in war and Louis would have seized the crown. John's death meant that Louis didn't have that opportunity.

- John's death removed the cause of the barons' rebellion. They had problems with John, not with his son Henry, who at just nine years old was untainted by his father's actions. Many barons preferred an English king to a French one.

- As Protector of the young King Henry, William Marshal proved a good ruler who provided good military leadership. He was also clever in reissuing Magna Carta: the rebel barons' original motive for going to war had been because John refused to agree to Magna Carta.

You might disagree with the statement with points like the following:

- Although Prince Louis and the barons were in the ascendency when John died, John still had powerful and influential supporters including William Marshal and most importantly the pope.

- The Church supported John and then his son Henry. By claiming the English crown, Louis would have been going against the Church, making it unlikely he would have become king.

- John had built up the English navy into a strong force. This proved decisive in military terms, as more troops from France would always have been needed to conquer the rest of England and the navy would have been able to stop them.

Notes

Notes

Notes

Notes

Notes

Notes

Published by Pearson Education Limited, 80 Strand, London, WC2R 0RL.

www.pearsonschoolsandfecolleges.co.uk

Copies of official specifications for all Pearson qualifications may be found on the website: qualifications.pearson.com

Text and illustrations © Pearson Education Ltd 2017
Produced, typeset and illustrated by Tech-Set Ltd.
Cover illustration by Eoin Coveney

The right of Kirsty Taylor to be identified as author of this work has been asserted by her in accordance with the Copyright, Designs and Patents Act 1988.

Content written by Rob Bircher, Brian Dowse and Victoria Payne is included.

First published 2017

20 19 18
10 9 8 7 6 5 4 3 2

British Library Cataloguing in Publication Data
A catalogue record for this book is available from the British Library

ISBN 978 1 292 17640 6

Printed in Slovakia by Neografia

Acknowledgements
The author and publisher would like to thank the following individuals and organisations for permission to reproduce photographs:

(Key: b-bottom; c-centre; l-left; r-right; t-top)

Alamy Stock Photo: age fotostock 20, Granger Historical Picture Archive 24, Josse Christophel 26; **Bridgeman Art Library Ltd:** British Library, London, UK 8, Pictures from History 16tr, Private Collection / © Look and Learn 27, Universal History Archive / UIG 16br; **Fotolia.com:** davidyoung11111 5, madiedu 29; **Mary Evans Picture Library:** J. Bedmar / Iberfoto 2

All other images © Pearson Education

Notes from the publisher
1.
In order to ensure that this resource offers high-quality support for the associated Pearson qualification, it has been through a review process by the awarding body. This process confirms that this resource fully covers the teaching and learning content of the specification or part of a specification at which it is aimed. It also confirms that it demonstrates an appropriate balance between the development of subject skills, knowledge and understanding, in addition to preparation for assessment.

Endorsement does not cover any guidance on assessment activities or processes (e.g. practice questions or advice on how to answer assessment questions) included in the resource, nor does it prescribe any particular approach to the teaching or delivery of a related course.

While the publishers have made every attempt to ensure that advice on the qualification and its assessment is accurate, the official specification and associated assessment guidance materials are the only authoritative source of information and should always be referred to for definitive guidance.

Pearson examiners have not contributed to any sections in this resource relevant to examination papers for which they have responsibility.

Examiners will not use endorsed resources as a source of material for any assessment set by Pearson.

Endorsement of a resource does not mean that the resource is required to achieve this Pearson qualification, nor does it mean that it is the only suitable material available to support the qualification, and any resource lists produced by the awarding body shall include this and other appropriate resources.

2.
Pearson has robust editorial processes, including answer and fact checks, to ensure the accuracy of the content in this publication, and every effort is made to ensure this publication is free of errors. We are, however, only human, and occasionally errors do occur. Pearson is not liable for any misunderstandings that arise as a result of errors in this publication, but it is our priority to ensure that the content is accurate. If you spot an error, please do contact us at resourcescorrections@pearson.com so we can make sure it is corrected.